YOUTH LEAGUE SOCCER

PROMOTING ATHLETICS · PHYSICAL EDUCATION · RECREATION

Athletic
Institute

SINCE 1934

COACHING AND PLAYING

The Athletic Institute
200 Castlewood Drive
North Palm Beach, Florida 33408
U.S.A.

Consultants
Soccer Association For Youth
Cincinnati, Ohio

George Beim, President
World Cup Sports, Inc.
Englewood, New Jersey

Demonstrators
Winnetka Park District Soccer Players
Tony Schinto, Coach

Cover Photo
Neal Morris

Library of Congress Catalog Card Number 81-70308

ISBN 87670-085-7

Introduction

Are you the coach of your town's little league team — a young player just starting out in this rigorous sport — a recently converted fan to this exciting game? Then this book is for you!

Coaches will love it because they'll learn the intricacies of managing a youth soccer team — including the philosophy, discipline and fundamentals of successful coaching.

Players will love it because they'll learn to master all the game's aspects — including the techniques of ball control, dribbling, passing, heading, goal keeping, tackling and much more.

Fans will love it because they'll become more involved spectators after familiarizing themselves with the rules of the game — all seventeen of them!

And there's more! Exercises, practice drill, principles of attack and defense, game formations, explanatory photos and illustrations. You don't have to be a strapping, big fellow to play the game well (in fact the small, agile guys often have the advantage), and you don't need expensive equipment or uniforms to start a team!

Are these the reasons why everybody's teaching it, coaching it, playing it and watching it? Find out! Read this book to learn more about the sport that's sweeping us by storm — and gaining momentum every day!

Contents

Philosophy

The Philosophy of Coaching

Soccer is one of the oldest games known to man and, by far, the most popular game in the world. Its penetration of the American sport scene has been delayed because the immense popularity of American football has pretty much crowded it off the sports calendar.

Two developments are generally recognized as having opened the door to soccer in this country. The rising cost of equipping and fielding a competitive school football team in an era of frozen school budgets has made team soccer a very attractive alternative. The cost of equipping a soccer player can be measured in pennies as compared with the equivalent cost in dollars of fielding a suitably equipped football player.

Further, soccer offers an opportunity for play by all youngsters, regardless of physical endowment. The smaller, agile boys or girls can compete on even terms with the bigger players, and often to their advantage. This elimination of the weight factor has contributed materially to the phenomenal growth in popularity of the game in the United States.

Soccer has a very special appeal. It is essentially an exercise in problem solving. The problem: How to penetrate the opponents' defense to score, and how to thwart an opponent's attack on your goal — and regain possession of the ball. The problem must be solved by superior skills. These basic skills include Passing, Dribbling, Ball Control, Heading and Shooting. Each of these skills may be mastered separately by drill and practice, but all fit together into patterns of attack and defense.

The role of the coach is to teach these skills and then, having developed the skills to their charges' peak potential, apply them to instilling in the players a "sense of movement" — a constant awareness on the part of the players of the flow of action. This is the development of a tactical sense which moves the players automatically and almost instinctively to his most effective position in the rapidly changing patterns of play because soccer is a fast-moving, uninterrupted action game calling for improvisation and anticipation.

The welfare of the players is the first responsibility of the intelligent volunteer coach. Even before the team takes the field for its first practice session, the coach must assure himself that each player is physically prepared to accept the stresses of the game. Has each candidate for play been certified as fit by a physician? And, as the season progresses, is each player in sound physical condition to compete?

Having satisfied himself on these counts, the coach will supervise all practice sessions carefully. He will see that an ample supply of drinking water is available and will watch carefully for any signs of exhaustion. He will familiarize himself with first aid procedures in case of injury, will learn to recognize the severity of an injury, and have ready access to medical help if the severity of an injury calls for it.

What to coach and how to coach it are among the first questions the soccer coach must answer. He will recognize that each practice must have a Positive result. Success builds confidence and great triumphs are erected on a solid foundation of small successes. The good coach will send each player away from the practice field with a reinforced sense of personal worth, of greater self-confidence.

He will add variety to his practice sessions to avoid the drudgery that erodes the enthusiasm of the player. Happily, soccer is a game in which, even mastery of the basic skills can be accomplished under competitive, game-like conditions. This book will offer a wide variety of drills that are spiced with the essential flavor of game conditions.

It is important for the coach to establish a happy rapport with his charges. All youngsters are not poured out of the same mold. They do not learn at the same rate, nor do they all respond to the same emotional stimuli. They have differing attitudes based on different life experiences and may mature at a different rate. Not all are motivated in the same way.

At first glance, it would appear a hopeless assignment for a coach to attempt to bring these wide-ranging personality differences together in a single homogeneous mass called a "team." But the wise coach will consider these differences, hope to recognize them as they appear, and react accordingly.

The wise coach also will realize that his association with his young charges can leave a lasting imprint on their characters and conduct himself accordingly, responding to situations on the practice and game field with maturity.

Meanwhile, the coach must accept the same standards of discipline that he demands of his players. If he sets a firm practice deadline of 2 p.m., he will be on the field at 1:45. And he must be prepared to make the same personal sacrifices that he is asking of his team.

Finally, he will listen and learn, constantly seeking to improve his own coaching techniques and his knowledge of the game just as he expects his youngsters to accept instruction and improve their skills.

The Responsibilities of a Volunteer Coach

Liability

Because they have volunteered their time, many volunteer coaches never stop to think that they are responsible for the welfare of the youngsters they coach. The feeling is that since they are donating their time they are not really held responsible. **Nothing could be further from the truth.**

Morally, the volunteer coach is held responsible for the psychological damage he may cause youngsters. Parents want him to see that proper attitudes are instilled in their youngsters' minds. The physical aspect is also important. Volunteers who agree to coach also agree to be responsible for the safety of the young people they coach. If proven negligent, coaches may be held liable for physical harm incurred by players in their charge.

Included in this section are areas about which a conscientious person will become informed before he begins working as a volunteer coach.

Physical examinations

All youngsters participating on the team should have a physical examination with written approval from a medical doctor stating they are physically fit to participate in athletic competition. **Don't take the chance of serious injury because you didn't take the time to see whether the player was medically fit!**

Field maintenance

It is your responsibility to regularly check the field for ruts, holes, rocks and other potential hazards.

Provide plenty of liquids for practice sessions and games

During exercise it is necessary to replace water loss (perspiration) hour by hour to help prevent heat exhaustion and dehydration.

How many games to play during the season

Many volunteer coaches get wrapped up in the thrill of coaching (especially if it's a winning team), so much so that they go and schedule extra games for the kids. Besides being unrealistic, it is unhealthy for a youngster to be involved in too many games and practices per season. Why? Here are a few reasons:

1. The strain of too many soccer games can drastically affect the overall system of a youngster during adolescence.

2. The psychological strain of winning and losing can take its toll on the emotional growth of a youngster.

3. Young people must have enough time for home, school and social responsibilities. Overemphasis on athletics can spark rebellion.

Know the rules

Agreeing to coach means you also agree to know the rules. A coach who "thinks" he knows the rules bcause he watches television on weekends is only fooling himsef. There is a big difference between pro rules and high school or youth league rules. Many games have been lost simply because a coach did not take the time to learn the difference.

4

Building Character As A Volunteer Coach

Using the concept that "a young person is at his learning best while at play," listed below are areas where the volunteer coach can be instrumental in developing lifelong attitudes in the young people he serves:

Desire

A young player acquires the will and courage to achieve in sports.

Social contacts

Young people have the opportunity to make new friends through sports participation. It also gives them confidence in the future.

Discipline

Learning to abide by training, practice and game rules teaches discipline. A good rule to follow — be firm, but fair.

Cooperation

Working together as a team instills in youth the importance of learning to get along with others. Winning teams seem to possess this quality — encourage it whatever the situation.

Emotional control

Emotional blowups only hamper an individual's success as an athlete, and he soon learns this. Your example can be very influential in this area.

Loyalty

Being faithful to a team, a group, a cause is an important lesson of athletics. A person will not fail himself when he has learned the lesson of being true to others.

Good physical condition

Healthy bodies are the result of conditioning for athletic competition.

Perseverance

The lesson **not to give up** is a valuable one learned when the going is tough. Young athletes can learn that slogans like "quitters never win and winners never quit" are still applicable in adult years.

Pressure adjustment

All athletic competitors are faced with thinking under pressure, whether it is a quarterback fading back to pass or a basketball player shooting an important free throw.

Care of Athletic Injuries

Did you ever stop to think that your actions in case of an injury could, in the most extreme case, save an individual's life or, in the mildest case, have your player back in action in a matter of minutes? Think about it — it's true.

The care of athletic injuries is a subject too vast and complicated to cover in total. However, our purpose in this publication is to inform you, the volunteer coach, as to the (1) practical equipment you should have on hand at all times, (2) the most common injuries in youth soccer and (3) the immediate **first-aid** steps to follow in case one of these injuries occurs.

Included in this section are areas about which a conscientious person will become informed before he begins working as a volunteer coach.

Practical needs

1. Most sporting goods stores carry regular **coach's first-aid kits.** As a check list, however, all coach's first-aid kits should contain:

- Adhesive tape — several different sizes for several purposes.
- Ammonia caps for dizziness.
- Antiseptic solution (betadine).
- Aspirin for simple headaches.
- Plastic bottles for carrying water.
- Cold packs.
- Elastic wraps of various sizes.
- Gause pads.
- Soap.
- Salt tablets for hot, humid weather.
- Scissors.
- Tongue depressors.
- Eyewash solution with eyewash glass.

2. The **telephone number of the nearest ambulance service** should be taped inside the first-aid kit. Always know where the closest available phone is at every game or practice site. Also tape a quarter to the inside of the first-aid kit, in case the closest phone is a pay phone.

3. Whenever possible **have a physician or nurse present.** A check with the players at the beginning of the season is an easy way to determine whether any parents are doctors or nurses. If any of them are, call and ask them for help during the season. They often are quite willing to help.

The basic approach in first aid

Always remain calm.
It's not easy, since the first sight of an injury can be upsetting. Nevertheless, helping to keep the injured player calm can sometimes be the best first aid you can render. This can only be accomplished if you remain calm yourself.

Never assume the role of a physican.
The old saying, "It is better to be safe than sorry," is one that intelligent volunteer coaches will heed. Whenever there is any doubt, refer to a physician.

Never move a player who has a serious injury.
This includes not sitting him up.

Use good judgment by stopping to think.

Never continue play of the game when a serious injury occurs.

Common injuries and immediate first-aid procedures

Nosebleed —
Have the player sit and apply cold to nose (ice cubes or cold cloth) while pinching pressure at the bridge of the bleeding side of the nostril.

Scrapes and burns —
Wash with cleansing solution that can be found in most coach's first-aid kits. Cover with clean gauze.

Unconscious player —
Do not move the player. Have one of your assistants call for an ambulance. Stay with the injured player and check to make sure that the breathing passages are clear.

Back injury —
If the pain is severe and numbness or weakness in the legs results, immediately send for an ambulance. Do not attempt to move the injured player. If the pain is slight, apply cold to the area.

Neck injury —
As with any back injury, do not attempt to move or sit the player up if the pain is severe, and especially if there is numbness or lack of feeling. Keep the injured player calm. Many times a head injury can be a neck injury; therefore, treat it accordingly.

Heat —
Heat prostration is the inability of the human body to cool itself rapidly enough to keep up with the heat reduced through exercise. In hot to humid weather the body cannot sweat and dissipate heat effectively. If an available source of water to replenish sweat is lacking, the problem is compounded.

Treatment should be directed at the immediate cooling of the body. Keep the player flat and move to a shaded, cool and well-ventilated area. If the player is responsive, small amounts of water may be given until an ambulance arrives.

Blisters —
Fluid accumulation between layers of skin due to friction. If the blister is intact, use a sterile needle to place a small hole at the base of the blister. Gently push the fluid from the blister. Leave the skin over the blister. This serves as a protective covering for the sensitive skin. If the blister is broken, remove the dead skin with sterile scissors and soak the area in warm, soapy water. Apply a sterile dressing with some antibiotic ointment.

Abbrasions —
A rubbing off of skin caused by sliding or falling. Wash the wound with unperfumed soap and water in order to remove any foreign matter. Wash it twice a day to continue to keep it clean. Also keep the wound exposed to the air as much as possible in order to promote healing.

Lacerations —
Jagged tearing of the skin and/or tissue. Any cut with marked bleeding

should be seen by a physician. Direct pressure will almost always stop bleeding. Clean the wound lengthwise with unperfumed soap and water and cover it with a sterile dressing. Suturing may be necessary especially if the wound is deep, if the cut is over a joint or on the foot or hand.

Bruises —
Blow to the body resulting in mild to severe pain with or without swelling. Ice, compressing with an elastic wrap and elevation. Use ice if there is no pain when walking, jumping, or running. The bruise may last for a couple of weeks. If the athlete cannot walk or run or move his foot after 24 hours, medical attention is indicated. Emergency treatment should be sought if the area begins to swell immediately or severe pain occurs. Shin guards should always be worn to prevent bruises to the lower leg.

Muscle cramps —
A severe pulling or cramping of any muscle in the body. Stretch the muscle until the pain is gone. If the cramp is in the calf, push the foot against an inmovable object until the pain is gone. If the pain is in the side of the abdomen, reach as high as possible with your hand on the affected side until the pain is gone. If the pain persists, it is better to rest and ice the muscle until the pain lessens.

Strains —
The athlete will feel a sharp, snapping sensation or pulling and will be able to point to the exact area of the strained muscle. The muscle will tighten and the athlete will slow down or be unable to continue participation. Ice the area, wrap with an elastic wrap, and elevate the injured part. No activity should be performed until there is absolutely no pain in the area. One does not "run off" these injuries! In other words, once a muscle is strained, chances are it will strain again if not properly treated.

Sprained ankle —
Swelling, tenderness, and bruising immediately around the front of the anklebone. Inability to move the ankle up and down and/or sideways. Ice, elastic wrap, elevation. To be on the safe side, I would suggest that an X-ray be taken to rule out any serious ligament damage or possible fracture. Athletes with any pain in the ankle should definitely not practice or play until the ankle is completely pain-free. NOTE: You should presume a fracture if your player is under twelve and has swelling, bruising, and tenderness over the ankle area.

Testicular trauma —
Blow to the male gential region with or without difficulty in breathing. He should be flat on his back with his knees bent and feet on the ground. Tell him to now breathe through his nose and exhale through his mouth as if he were blowing a whistle. This should slow down the rapid breathing. He can resume activity when he is ready. If he continues to have severe pain, you will have to check and see if there is any swelling in the scrotum and if both testicles are visible. If only one testicle is detected, the other may have been pushed up into the abdomen. This is an emergency situation. The testicle can be permanently lost if not properly treated at the emergency room. Ice should be applied to the scrotum if there is swelling in that area.

Wind knocked out —
Difficulty in breathing due to blow to solar plexus. Same procedure as the testicular trauma case using the nose-mouth breathing.

10

Discipline
of Coaching

A METHOD FOR PRACTICE

It is important that the coach have an awareness of the "essential nature" of the game of soccer and that the method of presenting the skills to his players be planned to promote a genuine understanding of this "essential nature."

What is the essential nature of the game? Perhaps a definition will help.

"SOCCER IS A PASSING AND RUNNING GAME OF UNPREDICTABLE AND CONSTANTLY CHANGING PATTERN, DEMANDING AN ACUTE AWARENESS OF OTHER PLAYERS AND AN ABILITY TO MAKE QUICK DECISIONS AND ACT UPON THEM WITHOUT DELAY."

If you further observe, that during a game, play is often confined to a limited space,or "tight situations" demanding quick and skillful control of the ball, you have probably gotten deep enough into its essential nature to decide what the priorities should be in teaching the game to your players.

The priorities, then, are the PROGRESSIVE ACQUISITION OF THE ESSENTIAL SKILLS (Passing, control, dribbling and challenging, heading and shooting) and BASIC TACTICS (movement with or without the ball in realistic situations demanding the making of decisions at every stage).

The practices in this manual have been carefully selected to help the coach to concentrate on these priorities. Study of these practices will reveal that they are not "coach dominated" drills, but realistic situations involving the players in problem-solving learning, and they include:

Progressive Acquisition of Essential Skills

The practices in this manual are progressive, that is, they are arranged in order of increasing difficulty, overloaded in the beginning to guarantee success, progressing to situations demanding a higher degree of skill.

A number of such situations are offered for each skill at every level of difficulty, so that the coach may add variety to the practice.

The order in which the skills are presented are: 1. Passing, 2. Control, 3. Dribbling and Challenging, 4. Heading, 5. Shooting and 6. Goalkeeping. This order is not random or haphazard. Each topic contains elements of skill and tactical awareness that are vital to the success in succeeding topics. For example, success in the second topic, Control, will depend on a reasonable degree of skill in the first topic, Passing.

As you progress in your practice and your players begin to display some skill in the small-side games, it is no longer absolutely necessary for the topics to be practiced in any particular order but, again, Passing will be the crucial topic on which success in the others will be built.

Realism

Practice conditions should closely resemble contest conditions as soon and as much as possible. To achieve this, opposition is necessary. Activities without opposition are of limited value. They do, however, have a place in the practice. Their chief purpose is to "groove" the movement pattern of a technique or skill before it is placed into a competitive situation. Very young players are more likely to practice such "grooving" than older ones. If this opportunity is missed, it will never return.

In this manual we have included activities without opposition, but they are linked at all times to more realistic practices with opposition. As skill level increases, practice without opposition will take up a progressively smaller amount of the practice.

FACTORS EFFECTING THE LEARNING OF SKILLS

It would be convenient if the acquiring of athletic skills followed a smooth and upward curve. Unfortunately it does not. It is affected by a number of factors which the coach should be aware of. They are:

Whole and Part Learning

Some skills, usually very simple ones, can be acquired by practicing them whole. Others are far too complicated and must be broken down into parts. The whole game of soccer, as we have seen, must be broken down into its parts. Fortunately, these parts can themselves be interesting and are easily put back into the whole game.

The principles behind the practices in this manual allow your players to enjoy participating in realistic parts in which they can be successful and which can be related to a whole they can also understand.

Transfer of Training

The progressive acquisition of game skills is dependent on the transfer of training from one situation to another. The guiding principle behind the practices in this manual are based on this transfer of training. They are arranged in such a manner as to promote "positive transfer effects," namely, the learning of one activity will facilitate the learning of the next.

Motivation

Most boys and girls enjoy playing soccer so that there are few problems in motivating them. However, if they are to progress in skills, they must enjoy and see the purpose of practicing the parts of the whole game. Soccer, as we have already observed, can be broken down into meaningful and enjoyable parts so that the problem motivation hardly arises.

We must emphasize the positive rather than the negative aspects of each individual performance. Situations should be planned, especially in the early stages of practice, to make your players feel successful. If they leave the practice with a feeling of pride rather than shame, they will continue to be attracted to soccer, they will be interested in discovering their weaknesses or mistakes and be willing to correct them. "What athletes believe about themselves is often more important than their actual ability."

Age

The age of your players will have an effect on the progressive acquisition of skills. Progress for children 6-8 years old will be much slower than with older groups. The important thing is not to give up. Stay with it! You will see improvement if you are patient and follow the concepts in this manual.

At about 9-10 years of age, most children really become enthusiastic about team sports and are prepared to practice hard to achieve success in them. This has been called "the golden age of skill learning" and lasts but a few years. The ability at this age to improve skills will begin to increase rapidly.

Individual Considerations

Individual differences among children will effect the learning of soccer skills. Keep in mind that:

1. All children do not learn at the same rate.
2. All children do not respond to the same instructional approach in the same way.
3. The greater the ideal presence of personal attributes associated with achievements, the greater the potential will be realized.
4. Personal limitations can be compensated for. For example, hustle can overcome certain deficits in size or skill.
5. Children have different motives, values, and interests.
6. Children have different experiences and dissimilar potential for athletic success.
7. Children mature at different rates, thus producing a dissimilar potential for learning.

Pondering these individual differences is enough to make a grown person shudder. How is it possible to reconcile all these differences and some how help every child to reach his or her athletic potential in the limited time you have to work with them? Let's be realistic. You can't. But you can think about them. You can be sensitive to these differences and alert to what they may mean in athletic potential and performance.

14

PLANNING YOUR PRACTICE
Explanation of the Practice Outline
Your practice should be divided into three parts:
- A.   OPENING ACTIVITY
- B.   SKILL TRAINING
  - 1.   Small group practice without opposition.
  - 2.   Small group practice with opposition.
- C.   GAMES

A. Opening Activity

The purpose of the opening activity is to allow your players to begin work immediately upon arrival at the practice area. As many balls as possible, ideally one for each player, should be available so that they can (a) practice freely with a ball or (b) practice a technique suggested by the coach, probably from work done in a previous session. These are generally simply organized activities and are essentially an introductory or "warm-up" stage of the practice that lead naturally into the next part of the practice plan. There should be ample score for free movement and vigorous activity so that the players are quickly warmed up. It is during this part of the practice that the players should be encouraged to develop their mastery of the ball, i.e. juggling and to improve their dribbling skills. Some suitable activities for this part of the practice are noted under CONTENT OF THE PRACTICE.

B. Skill Training

This is the main teaching part of the practice. During the first few practice sessions, you will want to concentrate on a particular skill, i.e. passing, and introduce a series of progressive practices for that skill (small group practice without opposition to small group practices with opposition.) Each aspect of the game is then taken up in successive practice sessions. Suitable practices for each topic are illustrated and described under CONTENT OF THE PRACTICE.

It is important that practices without opposition be carried out as near match speed as possible in order to give a sense of realism and to facilitate the "transfer" of skill to the practices with opposition.

Your role at this stage of the practice is vital. This is the part of the practice where you will find it necessary to demonstrate a particular skill or technique when introducing it to your team for the first time. A demonstration may also be needed when most of the team is making a particular mistake. If you are skillful, you can demonstrate the technique yourself. However, if you are not, you should use your most skillful players to give the demonstration. Above all, demonstrations should be good ones. They should be brief and should illustrate clearly one, or at the most, two points. They should not interfere with the flow of your plan and should always be followed by practice.

The development of skill and understanding will be determined by your ability to observe and correct faults as they happen. Your MANUAL contains illustrations for the proper techniques for each skill. You should study these techniques and practice them yourself. This will increase your ability to recognize faults and correct them.

Your intelligent observation is also needed to decide when to progress to another level of difficulty or when to consolidate one of the crucial and subtle arts of coaching is knowing when to make this decision, and this can only be learned through experience. Hopefully this manual will help to give you that experience.

C. Games

Games of various kinds should take up at least half of every practice. The games played should be a natural follow-up from the proceeding part of the practice and can be "conditioned" in order to focus the attention of the players and the coach on the particular aspect of the game that is being tackled. It is during this part of the practice that the players attempt to "transfer" the techniques and skill into actual games of soccer involving small numbers of players to a side. This transfer will be facilitated by the realistic nature of the SKILL TRAINING portion of the practice.

Deciding Where to Begin

The amount of time you spend on each stage of the practice, or how long you spend on a particular skill before progressing to another, should vary according to the level of ability of your players.

It might be convenient to start from scratch with Passers, and Wings, whatever their ability, and progress quite quickly to a more realistic level. With older and more skillful groups, you can quickly access their level of skill in a small-side game.

Thus, when a new aspect of the game is introduced, about half of the time in part B of the practice will be devoted to practice without opposition and the other half to practice with opposition. As skill level rises, more time will be devoted to practice with opposition until the whole of B of the practice is taken up with such practices. The balance will be restored when a new skill is introduced. This is a flexible plan whatever the length of your practice. The diagram in figure (1) shows the development of the practice outline during the teaching of a skill.

If you follow the suggestions about the order of presenting the skills and use your powers of observation and knowledge of children to decide when to progress, we are confident that your players will grow in skill and understanding and gain knowledge essential to playing the game.

Fig. (1)

A OPENING ACTIVITY
B SKILL TRAINING
C GAMES

1) without opposition
11) with opposition

STAGE 1: Introduction of new technique.

STAGE 2: As the players improve less time is devoted to techniques without opposition.

STAGE 3: Improvement continues and B (1) is reduced further.

STAGE 4: The whole of the skill is devoted to practices with opposition.

STAGE 5: Occasionally most of the lesson is devoted to games.

Pre-practice Checklist

1. **Practice Outline.**

   You will need a brief outline of your practice plan to help you remember the activities that you have chosen for your practice session.

2. **Soccer Balls.**

   Ideally there should be a ball for each player, or at the very least, one ball for every two players. The importance of this cannot be overstated. Probably your league does not provide you with a ball for each player. This can be overcome by stressing that each player bring his own soccer ball to practice.

3. **Grid Markers.**

   Many of the practices in this manual are organized around the use of the grid. You will need about twelve markers of some sort to use in setting up the boundaries of the grids. The ideal grid markers are cones used by highway departments, etc. Another excellent marker is the plastic bicycle safety flag. One can easily carry a dozen or so of these, and they are also excellent for making small goals used in many of the practices. Plastic jugs filled about one third with sand are excellent and inexpensive. The simplist form of grid marker is a tee-shirt that can be placed on the ground to mark the grid. Of course any combination of the above can be used.

4. **Colored Shirts.**

   Many of the practices require that the players be able to distinguish between teams. For this you will need six or eight colored shirts. You can provide them yourself, or you may want to have about half of your players always wear white or colored shirts to practice.

5. **Stop Watch.**

   Some of the practices are timed, and a stop watch or a watch with a second hand will be useful for this purpose.

The Use of The Grid

The grid is the foundation of many of the practices in this manual. It is a great method for teaching: a) execution of basics under pressure, b) improved passing, c) teamwork, d) basic tactics — movement with and without the ball.

The advantage of the grid is that it keeps the play confined to an area suitable for the activity being taught, allowing the players to "play" the ball many times under realistic conditions.

The grid is simply a confined area using four corner markers to mark the outside boundaries of the area. The size is varied according to the space required for a particular activity. A large grid is sometimes divided into zones or smaller grids simply by placing markers along its perimeter. The boundaries of the grid are then imaginary lines and can be changed easily by simply moving the markers.

Figure 2 illustrates how the internal markings of a regular soccer field can make convenient grids for many of the practices.

Fig. (2)

Coaching the Fundamentals

coaching the fundamentals

A good way to teach skill in soccer is in three progressive steps:

1. Introduce a specific technique and have the players practice it until they have achieved a reasonable degree of proficiency.

2. Introduce exercises that incorporate some movement of players and a limited degree of pressure from opponents to make the exercise related to match conditions.

3. Introduce exercises involving full pressure from opponents to simulate actual match conditions. Technique is the ability of a player to handle a soccer ball, but it does not become skill until the player can execute the technique under the pressure of match conditions.

Techniques Exercises
Juggling

Juggling is keeping the ball in the air through repetitive touches of the ball with any part of the player's body except the hands and arms. This juggling exercise can be of tremendous help in developing ball control since successful juggling requires proper contact of the ball. Through juggling players can work on their weaker foot and develop a good touch, balance and concentration.

1. ALWAYS KEEP EYES ON BALL.
2. EXTEND ARMS FOR BALANCE.
3. USE BOTH FEET, THIGHS, HEAD AND CHEST TO CONTACT BALL.
4. CONTACT BALL LIGHTLY TO MAINTAIN CONTROL.

Passing

The coach rolls the ball to a player who passes the ball back using the proper inside-of-the-foot technique.

Volleying

Three players stand in line facing the server who tosses balls to each player. The players volley the balls back. The server is changed after several volleys by each player.

Heading

Two players face each other and head a ball back and forth. To vary the exercise each player can be required to touch the ball twice with his head on each turn.

Dribbling under
Match-Like Conditions

Three players stand in a line about ten yards apart to act as
defenders. The dribbler tries to beat each of the defenders
one at a time. The defenders are allowed to move only laterally
in their attempts to dispossess the dribbler.

Heading under Match-Like Conditions

Two players face each other five yards apart. One player jogs backward while the other serves the ball for him to head back. The same exercise may be performed with the player who is heading the ball jogging forward.

Dribbling and Defending under Match-Like Conditions

A ball placed on the ground is the target. The offensive player uses another ball to attempt to hit the target for a point. The defender tries to gain possession of the ball, then goes on attack when he wins it. The game lasts two minutes.

Passing under
Match-Like Conditions

A grid ten yards x ten yards is set up with balls or other markers indicating the perimeter. A team of players has possession of the ball and must keep it away from one defender while staying within the square. The team players must move around to receive passes and elude the defender.

The same exercise may be used with two players to one defender, three players to two defenders and so on. Restricting players in possession to two consecutive touches of the ball increases the difficulty of the exercise.

Other Techniques Exercises

Other exercises can easily be devised. To make exercises more match-like, coaches may restrict the space in which to play and increase pressure from opponents. Other restrictions such as the number of consecutive touches of the ball allowed each player can make exercises more demanding and enable a coach to achieve specific goals. For example, a coach can force his players to make shorter passes simply by requiring that all passes be below the waist.

Conditioning Exercises

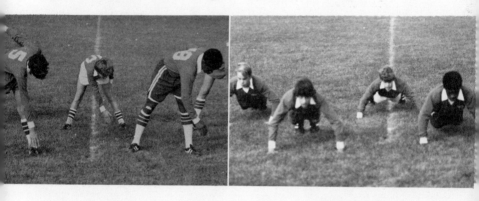

Proper warmups and conditioning are vital preparation for play. The following are sample exercises for small groups.

- Players jog with hands behind them, palms out, lifting their heels to touch their hands.

- Each player walks forward lifting his right foot to touch his outstretched left hand, then his left foot to touch the right hand.

- Each player stands to the side of a ball. With feet together he jumps laterally back and forth over the ball. For variation he may also jump forward and back over the ball.

- Each player stands with his legs straddled holding a ball overhead with arms extended. To a rhythmic count he touches the ball to the ground next to his left foot. After bringing the ball back overhead, he touches the ball to the ground next to his right foot and so on.

- Players sit on the ground with their legs outstretched. Each player rolls a ball along the ground around his back, around his outstretched legs and continuing around his back again.

- Each player lies flat on the ground on his back with legs straight and arms stretched out on the ground overhead. Each player has a ball between his feet which he lifts up and brings overhead to place in his hands. After the feet are brought back to the ground the ball is lifted with the hands and placed back between his feet. Players assume their original position and repeat the exercise.

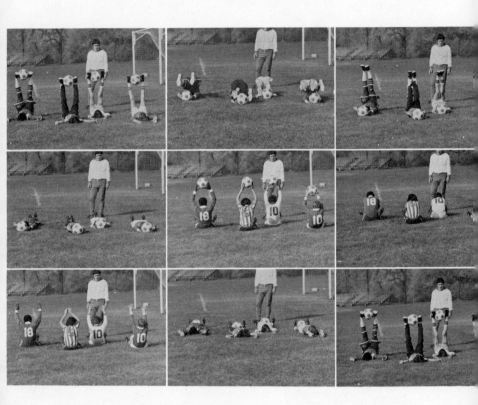

Tips for Soccer Players

1. Don't dribble when you can make a constructive pass.
2. Move to the open spot — move away from your defender — so you are in a better position to receive the ball.
3. When a defender is pressed and is in doubt as to what to do, kick the ball over the touchline.
4. When the ball is lost from view, all forwards should think defensively.

5. Make constructive passes to penetrate the opponents' defense, but if a penetrating pass is not possible pass to the side or back to a teammate.

6. Defenders can backpass to the goalkeeper as a safety maneuver. Pass to the outside of the goal mouth.

7. Make the easy play. Allow the ball to work for you. Don't work for the ball.

8. Wing forwards should stay wide and close to the touchline. This brings the defender out in the middle of the field and allows more open space for your attack.

9. Talk to your teammates on the field. Let them know what is happening in the area around them which their field of vision cannot pick up.

10. As a defender faced with two or more opponents, retreat slowly to allow teammates to come back to help. Always mark the defender who is closest to your goal.

11. Forwards should switch positions at various times during the game with other members of the forward line; for example, center forward with winger. This sometimes confuses the defense and creates passing opportunities.

12. Never retreat with your back to the ball. Watch the ball at all times.

13. As a defender, stay between ball and goal.

14. The closer the play develops toward your own goal, the tighter the defense.

15. As a good defender challenge only when you have a good chance to win the ball.

16. Defenders should exercise restraint and control. Let your opponent commit himself first.

17. Delaying principles are good tactics in defense. This means slowing down the opponents' forward line to regroup your own defense.

18. Back up teammates and help cover the space behind fellow players.

19. Always move toward the pass, don't wait for the pass to come to you.

20. A most important thing to learn is quickness off the mark. The first three or four steps are all-important in soccer. Beat your opponent to the ball.

21. What you do without the ball is as important as what you do with the ball.

22. Shoot first-time.

23. Play the ball, not the man.

Practice Drills

CONTENT OF THE PRACTICE

Key to Diagrams

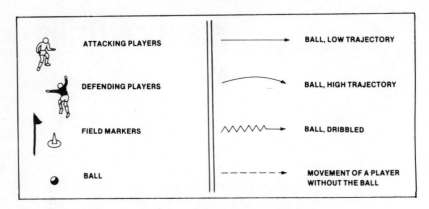

ATTACKING PLAYERS

DEFENDING PLAYERS

FIELD MARKERS

BALL

BALL, LOW TRAJECTORY

BALL, HIGH TRAJECTORY

BALL, DRIBBLED

MOVEMENT OF A PLAYER
WITHOUT THE BALL

First Topic: PASSING

Passing is the foundation on which the structure of soccer is built. Everything else that follows will involve this fundamental skill. Most experts agree that the coach should concentrate on the short pass with beginning players using the inside and outside of the foot. These are the most common passes used even in adult games. Through the "short game" your players will learn the value accurate passing and will not be tempted to "big foot" the ball to get themselves out of trouble.

Study your COACHING MANUAL for the proper techniques so that you will be able to recognize faults as they occur. Encourage your players to use either foot during passing practice.

Practice Without Opposition

1) **Passing In Pairs.**
   Two players passing one ball among themselves. Use inside and outside of feet. **Good Opening Activity.**

2) **Pass To Each Other's Balls.**
   Players in pairs, each with a ball. They take turns passing to partner's ball. Each touch counts one points.

3) **Pass Through The Legs.**

Players in pairs with one ball. They take turns attempting to pass the ball through partner's legs. If successful, counts one point.

4)   Pass Between the sticks.

Two players passing through the sticks. Stop and pass or first time pass. When it gets too easy, make the goals smaller or increase distance.

5)   Passing with two balls.

Two players, each with a ball, passing to each other. Can be done stationary or while moving. **Good Opening Activity.**

6)   Hot Potato.

6-8 players in a circle, passing the ball around as quickly as possible. Whoever has the ball at the end of the time limit is eliminated. Last player left is the winner.

7)   Soccer Golf.

Create a number of golf holes, using flags or cones, in a specific area. Players must hit the target at each hole. Count the strokes. Allow enough distance between starts.

8)   Pass and Follow.

The players must pass the ball to the target line with such pace that he catches up to the ball precisely at the target line. One point for each successful attempt.

9) Pass and run to Stick.

Groups of six to eight players. Player with the ball passes to anyone and sprints to the empty stick.

10) Pass and Follow.

Groups of six to eight players. Pass to anyone and follow your pass as fast as possible.

11) Circle Passing.

The players outside pass the ball to the man in the middle who must pass it back accurately. Can be done by stopping the ball or by first-time passing.

12) As above.

But now one player on each side of the circle is w/out a ball. When man in the middle receives the ball, he must control it and play it to the man without the ball. He turns and receives the ball from the other side etc. Variation: Now he receives a ball from the side he is facing, turns and plays it to the other side to the man without a ball.

36

13) Pass and Shoot.

First line of players starts out toward the goal. Before the shot is taken, every player must have touched the ball at least once. The team that shoots (or scores) in the least amount of time is the winner. Variation: The pass cannot go to the player next to the passer, yet every player must touch the ball as before.

14) Pass and Change Lines.

First player in line A passes to the first player in line B, then sprints to the end of the line B. First player in line B stops the ball and passes to the second man in line A etc. After awhile, try first-time passing.

15) Four line Passing.

As above, but now there are four lines of players passing among the lines with two balls. Players must be alert and keep their heads up to avoid collisions.

16) Wall Passing.

A passes to B who passes to A1 who passes to B1 who passes to C who passes to D etc. Use one-time passing.

37

Practice With Opposition

1) Passing with two balls.

Two teams of different colors, 3-5 players to a side in a limited area. Each team has a ball which they must pass amongst themselves. Count all the mistakes. Later, use an extra player as an opponent, trying to steal the ball from either team. May increase pressure by adding more opponents.

2) Monkey in the Middle.

Players on the outside pass the ball around w/out the insider(s) touching it. Can vary from 3 vs. 1 to 8 or 9 vs. 2. **Good Opening Activity.**

3) 3 vs. 1 To a Stick

A, B and C are trying to pass among themselves with the idea of hitting the stick with the ball. The defender is trying to prevent this. Change roles.

4) Through the neutral zone.

3 vs. 1 on each side of the neutral zone. A's must attempt to get the ball to their teammates A1's and vice-versa. Requires moving into a good receiving position away from the defenders. No player is allowed in the neutral zone.

38

5) Mark closely.

Mark a limited area with cones or flags. The defender is marking 'A' closely who is trying to pass the ball through the cones to B. If he succeeds, the defender must turn and mark B etc. One point for each successful pass. Alternate defenders.

6) Through the cones.

In a limited area, A's and B's are teams with different colors. Game is 3 vs. 3 and, if the ball is passed through the cones, a goal is scored. A's may use the A's in the other zone for passing combinations, but all the players must stay within their own zone. Also may award extra points for X-number of consecutive passes.

7) Soccer cones.

5-YDS		5-YDS
♣	2 VS. 2	♣
♣	UP TO	♣
♣	5 VS. 5	♣
♣		♣

Play anything from 2 vs. 2 to 5 vs. 5 (depending on size of the area). Teams are different colors and each team has a 5 yard zone with X-number of cones. First team to knock down all their cones is the winner.

8) Through the zones.

In an area approx. 20 x 40 yds., there are 4 zones. A's try to keep possession by interpassing through the B zone. If players B intercept the ball, or the A's kick it out of bounds, then the B's will try to keep possession by inter-passing through the A zone. Count successful through passes.

39

9) Wall pass game.

4 vs. 4 in a limited area. Two teams of different colors. A goal is scored if the team in possession passes the ball to their resting teammates and receives a return (one-time) wall pass. On command the workers rest and vice-versa.

10) 3 vs. 3 vs. 3 passing.

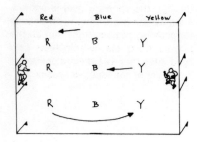

The blue team attacks the red team and tries to score. If the goalie saves, or the red team intercepts, then the red team attacks the yellow team while the blue team rests. When the yellow team gains possession, they will attack the blue team while the red team rests.

11) 4 goal game.

Two teams of equal numbers and different colors. The teams can score into any goal by passing the ball through a goal to his own teammate. Variation: Defend two goals and attack two.

11) Get free for a Pass.

1 vs. 1 in the middle. The forward must get rid of the defender to be free for the pass. He now calls a name and passes the ball right back to the same person. Use a time limit, or see how long it takes to get a pass from everybody.

12) Count the Passes.

6 vs. 6 to 8 vs. 8 in an area about 30 x 50-60 yds. Different colors. No goals. Team in possession can score a point by putting together X-number of consecutive passes (Inexperienced players — 3 passes in a row, experienced player — 5 or more). The object is to keep possession. If the opposing team intercepts, then try to do the same. May not get a pass back from the person you have just passed to. Encourage players to spread out and use the entire area. Variation for younger players: Use an extra player or two, and they are always on the team in possession of the ball.

13) As above.

But now add goalkeepers at each end of the field. A pass to your own goalkeeper now counts in the sequence of consecutive passes. The goalkeeper distributes the ball to one of his teammates, by rolling or throwing, to continue the count. The addition of the goalkeepers will encourage back passing and the players will become aware of the fact that the goalie is not just someone who stops goals.

41

Second Topic: CONTROL

Ball control is the ability to stop or change the direction of the ball coming out of the air, a ball bouncing at various heights, or a ball rolling along the ground. The ball must be controlled in such a manner that the player can do anything the situation requires; pass first time, stop and pass, stop and dribble, or shoot.

During a game, balls will be coming from all angles, speeds, spins and directions and a player is often required to bring the ball under control while under pressure, in heavy traffic, and perhaps running at high speeds or off balance.

Ball control is a skill that requires superb reflexes, balance and body control and takes many years to perfect. Youth soccer coaches should be very tolerant of mistakes in this area and realize that skill must be developed over many seasons of play.

The types of control most likely to be used are:
1. Use of the inside of the foot to take the pace off a ball rolling along the ground.
2. Use of the inside of the foot to take the pace off a low bouncing ball.
3. Use of the instep to take the pace off a low bouncing ball.
4. Use of the thigh to take the pace off a dropping ball.
5. Use of the chest to take the pace off a dropping ball.

Important points to stress while practicing control are:
1. Go to the ball. If not, an opponent will get it.
2. Position the body directly in the flight path of the ball.
3. Decide what type of control to use as the situation demands.
4. At the moment of ball contact, relax the part of the body contacted by the ball, so that the ball drops softly to the ground ready for any situation.

Again, study your COACHING MANUAL for the various techniques of ball control.

Practice Without Opposition

1) **Control in Pairs.**
One ball between two players 8-10 yds. apart. Players pass the ball firmly along the ground. They control it with the inside of the right or left foot and return it along the ground. **Good Opening Activity.**

2) **Against a Wall.**
Each player with a ball kicking it against a wall at various heights and speeds to practice control, This is an excellent activity for any age player and they can be encouraged to practice this also at home. **Good Opening Activity.**

3) Control in a square.

Players on the outside of the square toss different types of serves to the player in the middle. One point for each successful control. Player inside must control the ball to the ground and pass back to the server. After so many trys, change player in the middle.

4) Control and pass.

Two lines of players facing each other about 10 yds. apart. One line plays goalkeeper and tosses the ball to the first player in the other line. That player controls the ball, passes it to the next goalkeeper in the other line, and sprints to end of that line. Goalkeeper goes to the end of the control line.

5) Control in a circle.

Groups of 6-8 players in a circle and each with a ball. They take turns serving to player in the middle who must control the ball and pass it back to the server. Change player in the middle.

6) Ball Juggling.

Every player with a ball. Use various parts of the body (instep, thigh, head etc.) to keep the ball from touching the ground after it is tossed in the air. Have players keep count of successful attempts within a time limit. Player with the most consecutive touches is the winner. With younger players we can allow one bounce between juggles. **Good Opening Activity.**

7) Ball control relay race.

Two lines of players about 10-15 yds. from coaches. Coaches throw the ball to first player in their line. Players control the ball then dribble around the flag and return the ball to the coach. First team to finish is the winner.

8) Control and shoot.

In front of a goal, a line of players is outside the penalty area. Coach(s) serve the ball from either side of the goal. Player controls the ball and shoots at goal. If he misses, he must chase and return the ball to the coach before going to the end of line.

9) Control and turn.

Groups of three players. Player in the middle faces player A who serves him a ball which he must quickly control and return. Now he turns and receives a ball from player B etc. On command, change man in the middle.

10) Throw - Control - Catch.

6 to 8 Players To A Square

Two teams of equal numbers in adjacent squares. To start the game, a player in one square throws the ball to a teammate who controls it out of the air, with an appropriate method, and then catches it in his hands. He throws on to another teammate who controls and catches it etc. If the ball touches the ground, it is awarded to the other team in the other square. Variation: as above, but now the ball may not be caught with the hands at all. May allow two or three touches out of the air before passing on.

11) Two-touch game.

Two players with one ball. To start, one player tosses the ball up and controls it with one part of his body (head, chest, thigh, feet) and then passes it out of the air to his partner who controls it with an appropriate method and passes it back, etc. **Good Opening Activity** for older players. May be done in 3's.

Practice With Opposition

It is more difficult to isolate the practice of ball control into small groups with opposition, especially for younger groups. Many ball control skills will be developed in the GAMES portion of the practice because the players will be placed in small game situations with opposition where ball control is essential to the success of the game.

1) Control in a circle with opposition.

Same as number 5 above, but now there are two players inside the circle. As the ball is served, one player controls the ball as the other one attempts to steal it. Change roles.

2) Control and shoot with opposition.

As in number 8 above. But now you have a goalkeeper and when the coach serves the ball, the goalkeeper must come out and challenge the player trying to control and shoot.

3) Juggling with a hunt man.

Groups of 4-6 players juggling the ball with one player in each group without a ball. Whenever one of the players juggling the ball loses it, the player without the ball can now steal the ball. The player who lost the ball now becomes the hunt man.

4) Control and pass with opposition.

Same as number 4 above but now first player in line A serves the ball to the first player in line B, then runs to challenge. Player in line B must control the ball quickly away from the challenger in order to pass the ball back to the second man in line A. If he is successful or if the challenger gets the ball, the challenger will move to the end of line B and the controller will move to the end of line A etc.

Third Topic:
DRIBBLING AND CHALLENGING

Dribbling is an important skill and must not be discouraged, because doing so would take away individualism which the players will need later on. It must be stressed, however, that dribbling is not a substitute for a constructive pass and we should use our dribbling skills to: 1) hold the ball because there are no teammates free to pass to and 2) get past an opponent in order to pass to a teammate or shoot on goal.

Points to stress while practicing dribbling:
1) Use your feet to push the ball gently in front of you so that you are in control of it at all times.
2) When challenged, use your body as a shield to protect the ball.
3) Learn to fake your opponent by practicing changing speed, changing direction, stopping and fainting.
4) When dribbling, practice using your peripheral vision to locate the position of your teammates and opponents.

Most children are capable, even in the early stages, of making a reasonable effort to gain possession of the ball. Until now we have not stressed challenging because the emphasis has been placed on developing the skills of passing and control. Now we can concentrate also on challenging, because the nature of the dribbling exercises with opposition require that the dribbler "take on" an opponent.

Practice Without Opposition

1) **Follow the Leader.**

Groups of 3 or 4 players. Use your best dribblers as leaders. The line of players follows the leader and tries to imitate him the best they can. **Good Opening Activity.**

2) **Mass Dribbling.**

Everyone has a ball in the center circle, or any defined area, and they are looking for open spaces in which to dribble as the coach encourages them to change speed and direction. **Good Opening Activity.**

3) As above, but now the coach holds up his hand with a certain number of extended fingers. The players must use their peripheral vision and call out the correct number of extended fingers.

4) As above, but on command from the coach, the players must stop the ball and place a particular part of their body on the ball. (i.e. left foot, chin, right elbow, left ear etc.)

5) As above, but on command everybody exchanges balls.

6) **Red Light, Green Light.**

"It" is facing the finish line while a group of players are at the starting line. When "it" calls "green light", they start dribbling toward the finish line until he calls "red light" and everybody must stop. "It" then turns around, and if he sees someone moving, the player caught must go back to the starting line. "It" now calls "green lignt" and everybody starts dribbling again. Whoever reaches the finish line first, wins.

7) **Run For Your Cover.**

In a circle, "It" dribbles around the circle. When he stops between two players, they must now dribble as fast as they can around the circle in opposite directions. "It" takes one of the vacant spots while the fastest dribbler takes the other one. The slower dribbler now becomes "it" and must stop between two other players etc.

46

8) Dribbling to the base and back.

On command, everybody dribbles to the base and back. The slowest (or fastest) gets to the starter. Everybody must hit their cone or flag at the baseline.

Practice With Opposition

1) Tag.
Everyone has a ball in a limited area. One person is "it" and tries to tag the other players within the confined area. The taged player becomes "it". Can play points or letters and words. Note: "It" must not leave his ball to tag another player, and all players must stay within the confined area.

2) Kick the Ball Out.
Everyone is dribbling in the center circle or any confined area, but now the players are allowed to kick the other players' ball out of the circle. One must not leave his ball in order to go and kick another player's ball out of the circle. When a player loses his ball, he is out. The last player left with a ball wins.

3) Tag a Player with the ball.
Everyone in a defined area but only one player has a ball to start. He tries to hit the other players w/out a ball with his ball. Whoever gets hit must now go get their ball and join in. The number of players without a ball thus decreases, while the number of players dribbling increases.

4) Cranes and Crowes.

Two teams have starting lines 10-15 yds. apart in the middle of a marked area. Each team has a safety zone, and when either name is called, they must dribble to their safety zone. The other team must leave their balls and try to catch them before they reach the safety zone. Keep score of the most people caught.

47

5) Get your Ball.

In a marked area, put two less balls in the middle than there are players. (Two players will always end up without a ball.) On command "go" everybody tries to secure a ball and dribble back to their starting line. The two players who do not have a ball will try to kick away as many balls as possible. Those who lose their ball will join in the hunt. Count one point for each ball brought to safety.

6) Tornados and Stars.

On a regular soccer field, two teams of equal numbers and different colors are dribbling in the center circle. On command, the team called upon dribbles toward the opponent's goal while the other team leaves their balls in the center circle. The team in possession tries to score while the other team tries to prevent it. If the team without the ball gains possession, they try to bring the ball back to the center. This creates a number of one-on-one situations all over the field. An additional condition: Must shoot inside the penalty area.

7) Steal The Bacon.

Two teams of equal numbers facing each other about 15-20 yds. apart. Coach gives players across from each other the same number. When the coach calls a number, the two players run to get possession of the ball and dribble across their own safety line. Each successful attempt counts as a point. Ball must be dribbled over the safety line — not kicked.

As above, but now there are two goalkeepers defending two small goals. When the coach calls out a number the two players come and and play 1 vs. 1 in order to score. Duration of the exercise is 20-60 seconds. Coach has extra balls to throw in. Each goal counts one point.

9) As above, but now call out two or three numbers to create 2 vs. 2 or 3 vs. 3 situations, and they can use the players on the outside for wall passes before shooting.

10) Three 10 Yd. Squares.

A player starts dribbling through the three zones trying to beat each defender who can move from the back of his square only after the attacker enters that square. The defender cannot enter any other square. The attacker gets 1 point for each beaten defender, and 2 points for scoring a goal. (Variations are: 1) only two squares and 2) vary the size of the squares.)

11) Faking behind the line.

One player has the ball and tries to fake the defender out of his position and get to either marker ahead of the defender. The defender's job is to stay with the attacker. The defender **cannot** tackle the ball or cross the line. After awhile, change roles.

12) 1 vs. 1.

Players are in pairs with one ball. One player is dribbling and trying to shield the ball from his partner. One minute time limit. Change roles.

13) 1 vs. 1 with player resting.

Groups of three players with one ball. A is dribbling and shielding from B, while C is resting. When B gains possession, C tries to get it from B while A is resting etc.

14) Same As Above.

But now the resting player C has his legs spread apart and A and B are trying to score through his legs. As soon as the ball goes through C's legs, Player A becomes the goal etc. Count one point for each goal.

15) 1 vs. 1 to a ball.

One player is dribbling and shielding from his partner, trying to hit the stationary ball. If his partner steals the ball, then **he** tries to hit the stationary ball. Count each successful attempt as a goal. Play a time limit.

16) 1 vs. 1 around a stick.

Player A is dribbling and trying to stay behind the stick. Player B is trying to tag him. As soon as he does, they change roles. Player B may or may not have a ball.

17) Winterbottom 1.

Groups of four players. The players resting serve as goals by having their legs spread apart. Players in the middle play 1 vs. 1 and try to score through resting players' legs. On command "change", the players change roles. If the ball is lost, the resting players play one of the spare balls in.

18) Winterbottom 2.

Same as above, but instead of playing the ball through the legs, the workers must receive a return pass from the resting players, which counts as a point.

Fourth Topic: HEADING

Heading is not an easy technique for young players to acquire. The reluctance of many children, and even older players, to head the ball can very often be traced back to painful early attempts to head a heavy ball. It is important that dry, light, well-inflated balls be used for heading practice. Fortunately, with the new synthetic materials now being used, this is usually not a problem.

Points to stress when practicing heading:
1. Keep your eyes open and on the ball.
2. Strike the ball with the forehead. The ball is hit with a forward "snap" of the upper body, moving the head, neck and trunk of the body through the ball as one unit.
3. When heading from a standing position, feet should be placed one in front of the other for balance and power.

Practice Without Opposition

1) **Head To Your Partner.**
One ball between players about 5 yards apart. The player with the ball, holds it in front of him at head height. He heads it out of his hands to his partner, who controls it with a suitable technique before heading it back in the same way.

2) **Toss and Head to Your Partner.**
As above, but now the player in possession, throws the ball a few feet above and just in front of his head. He heads to his partner from a standing position. His partner controls it and returns it in the same manner.

3) As above, but now the players will toss the ball up, take a couple of strides, jump and head the ball to each other. All of the above are **Good Opening Activities.**

4) Heading in pairs for goals.

Goalkeeper throws ball to partner who tries to head it back through the small goal. Each take 10 attempts.

5) Circle heading with man in the middle.

All players in the circle have a ball. They serve alternately to player in the middle who must head back to them. Variation: must head back to their feet.

6) Head juggling.
Everybody with a ball. They start by tossing the ball up and trying to keep the ball in play with their head. Have players count successful attempts within a time limit. **Good Opening Activity** for older players.

7) Throw - head - catch.

Groups of three players with one ball. A serves to B who heads to C who catches. C now serves to A who heads to B who catches. etc.

8) Head for goal.

Using a regulation goal, coaches serve balls rapidly and alternately from just outside the goalpost. Players have to head for goal quickly and turn for next service. May vary distance from goal. May or may not have a goalkeeper.

9) Heading in threes.

Outside players each have a ball. Player A serves ball to B who must head it back and quickly turn to head a ball from C. etc. Change man in the middle.

10) As above.

But only with one ball. A heads to B, B heads back to A, A then heads over top of B to C. C heads to B who has turned to face him. B to C, C over top to A. Repeat.

11) Heading in two's.

One ball between two players. They are keeping the ball in play by heading in back and forth. May play one or two touch. **Good Opening Activity** for older players.

Practice With Opposition

1) 3 vs. 1

In a square approx. 10 yds, it is 3 vs. 1. The server serves the ball to anyone of his colleagues so that he can return it with his head without jumping. The three then try to make X-number of consecutive passes with their feet. When they have done that, or when the opponent gets the ball, the practice is repeated, the ball being served by whoever is in possession of the ball. Practice continues until each player has been both a receiver and an opponent.

2) Head for a goal w/opposition.

Same as in #8 above, but now there is a goal keeper. As soon as the coach serves the ball, the goalkeeper comes out to challenge the shooter who is trying to head the serve into the goal.

3) 6 vs. 6 Throw and Catch.

Two teams of equal numbers and different colors in an area about 20 x 40 yds. with a small goal at each end. Team in possession tries to advance the ball towards the opponents goal by passing the ball with their hands. In order to score, the ball must be headed into the goal from the pass. Opponents may catch the ball at anytime with their hands and attack the other goal in the same manner.

4) Throw · Head · Catch.

Same set up as above but now the sequence is throw-head-catch. The team in possession must advance the ball towards the opponent's goal in following manner: Player in possession throws the ball to a teammate with his hands. Teammate then heads the ball on to another teammate who catches it, throws to another teammate who heads it etc.

The defense may catch the ball in their hands at any time, but then they must throw-head-catch to advance the ball toward the opponent's goal. If the sequence is broken, the ball is turned over from the attacking team to the defending team. Goals can only be scored with a header.

Fifth Topic: SHOOTING

It is important that the players learn from the beginning to use their **instep** for shooting. Important points to remember are: **power** and **accuracy.** Study your COACHING MANUAL for the proper technique for shooting.

Practice Without Opposition

1) Shoot to your Partner.

Players in pairs punting the ball back and forth using their instep. Vary distance according to age level. Have them concentrate on keeping their toe pointed as they strike the ball with their shoe laces (instep). Should try to shoot into their partner's hands.

2) Half Volley to Partner.
Use same technique as above, but drop kick (half volley) ball to your partner.

3) Shoot a moving ball.

Players in pairs with one ball. Player A rolls ball on the ground player B who shoots the ball back to player B with instep. Change roles after X-number of tries.

4) Volley into goal.

Line of players in front of a regular goal. Each player has a ball in his hands. One at a time, they run toward the goal and shoot (volley) ball into goal using same technique as in #1.

5) Half Volley into goal.
Same as #4 but with drop kick (half volley).

6) Shooting a moving ball into goal.
As in #4 but now player rolls the ball in front of him, runs after it, and shoots from proper distance at the goal. Could now introduce a goalkeeper.

7) Shooting a bouncing ball.

Second player in line tosses the ball over the 1st player's head. 1st player runs on to the ball and shoots a goal.

8) Penalty Kick contest.
Each player has a ball and they take turns shooting penalty kicks. If a player misses the goal, he must sprint after the ball, and if he catches up to it before it stops rolling, he can stay in the contest. May have a goalkeeper.

9) Shoot Quickly.

Place 10 balls at specific locations in the penalty area. One player at a time attempts to shoot all balls into the goal while being timed. Add 5 seconds for every goal missed. The spoting of the balls may vary according to the skill level and strength of the players. May have goalkeeper.

10) Pass · Run · Shoot.

Line of players, each with a ball. First player in line plays a pass to target player, who controls the ball and lays it off for shooter to run on to and shoot. Target player now goes to the end of the shooting line and the shooter becomes the target man. May have goalkeeper.

11) Volley for Goal.

Line of players in front of a regular goal. First player in line moves to front edge of the goal box. Coaches serve balls from each side of the goal and player tries to volley ball into goal. Each player gets X-number of tries. May have goalkeeper.

12) Dribble and Shoot.

Two lines of players in front of goal with goalkeeper. First line of players dribble, one at a time, to appropriate distance and shoot at the goal. Then the second line gets their turn. The line that scores 5 goals first wins.

13) Control - Shoot - Turn.

Two goals are placed about 30 yds. apart. Balls are served from behind each goal alternately. Player can volley or control and shoot. Change shooter after X-number of balls. Use goalkeepers.

Practice With Opposition

1) 1 vs. 1 up to 4 vs. 4 in the penalty area.

Divide your team into two teams with different colors. Play will be inside the penalty area with a goalkeeper who is confined to the six-yard area (goal box). The coach has a pile of balls outside the penalty area on either side of the goal. The coach plays a ball into the penalty area and a player from each team will run to the ball from a point equal distant from the penalty area and play 1 vs. 1 trying to score. If a player scores, or the ball is kicked outside the area, or the goalie saves, the players will leave it and look to the coach who will toss in another ball. Each pair will play for one minute until all have had a turn.

Now continue the game, playing 2 vs. 2, 3 vs. 3, up to 4 vs. 4 with both teams trying to defend and score on the same goal. Variation: May require X-number of passes by a team before shooting.

Sixth Topic: GOALKEEPING

The position of goalkeeper is unique. It involves quite different techniques from outfield play. Some players, from an early age, show a particular aptitude for goalkeeping, other show a passing interest before returning to outfield play. In the beginning, all of your players should be given the opportunity to play goalkeeper in practice.

The activities in the previous topics were arranged so that the position of goalkeeper could be integrated into the main body of the practice. Now you can concentrate on the specific skills of goalkeeping involving the whole team.

What is goalkeeping?
"Goalkeeping is the ability to provide quick, correct responses to a number of simple problems."

In general there are five areas of responsibility:
1. Dealing with shots-saves. (catching and punching)
2. Dealing with crossed balls. (catching and punching)
3. Supporting the defense. (communication with back players)
4. Distributing the ball. (punting, throwing, rolling)
5. Defending at set plays. (corner kicks, penalties, free kicks)

Attributes of a good goalkeeper:

Physical
1. Strength
2. Elasticity
3. Quickness
4. Special skills (good hands, and diving ability)
5. Supple body
6. Good fitness

Psychological
1. Courage
2. Ability to relax
3. Concentration
4. Sense of game tempo
5. Ability to read the game
6. Calmness
7. Willpower and confidence

Goal Keeping Practice

1) Players in pairs throwing the ball to each other to practice secure handling of the ball. One point is scored everytime the ball is dropped.

2) Players in pairs kicking the ball to each other to practice punting and catching. In case of a bad kick or a dropped ball, a point is scored. Vary the distance according to the size and strength of the players.

3) **As Above.**
   But now the players are throwing into a small goal, thus the players can practice diving as well. A point is scored when the ball goes through the goal.

4) As above.

But now the ball is kicked. This exercise can also be done in three's. A tries to score on B, B tries to score on C, etc.

5) Save and Turn.

Players in 3's. A and B will shoot the goalie alternately. Points are scored for saves and goals. Players may rotate if necessary.

6) Turn Around.

Players in pairs. The goalkeeper has his back turned to the shooter (or thrower). The goalie turns around on command and tries to save the ball.

7) Push through the legs.

Two goalkeepers are facing each other with their legs spread apart. One goalkeeper pushes the ball through his partner's legs. As soon as the ball goes through, he tries to turn and fall on it. Every successful fall counts as a point.

8) Shooting exercise.

In front of a regular goal, at the proper distance, players shoot at the goalkeeper one at a time in quick succession. The goalkeeper must make a series of quick saves.

9) Up and down.

The goalkeeper is sitting down (or lying down) at the goalpost. On command, he must get up quickly and save a thrown or kicked ball. He must now go to the other post and repeat. Duration: 4-8 balls.

10) Post to post and over.

Server 1 throws ball to near post. He must throw it high. Goalie comes to tip it over the bar, and immediately turns to go to the other post to tip a ball over from server 2.

11) Same as above, but now goalkeeper must punch the ball. Later, add a challenging forward. Must punch it over the challenger's head.

12) **Two goalies on the goal line.**
The server throws a ball into the goal mouth and the two goalies fight for the ball. Each catch counts as a point. Variation is to punch the ball.

13) **Shoot and follow.**

Server 1 shoots from about 6-10 yds. The goalie tries to make a save as player A follows in for rebound, (in case goalie misses). Now server 2 shoots and player B follows in for rebound. Duration depends on the fitness level of the goalie(s).

14) 6 vs. 6 up to 8 vs. 8 playing regular soccer on a small field, but with no goals. The object of the game is to get the ball to the goalkeeper, which counts as a goal.

15) **Three goal game.**

Two goalkeepers must cover three goals. Field players can play 3 vs. 3 up to 5 vs. 5 trying to score as many goals as possible. This will teach the goalkeepers to be alert constantly.

16) **Four goal game.**

4 VS. 4 up to 7 VS. 7.

In a limited area, play up to 7 vs. 7. The two teams can shoot at any of the four goals as the exercise is for goalkeepers. If a goalie makes a save, he either punts or throws the ball into the midfield.

Practicing Crosses

The most dangerous crosses come from the goal line because this forces the goalkeeper to the forward square. This restricts the goalkeepers field of vision tremendously. When a cross comes from the touchline, the field of vision is much better. No matter where the ball comes from, it is always the goalies responsibility to cut the high crosses out.

On corner or goal line crosses, the goalie should stay about 1 yd, off the post and 2 yds. out of the net. This makes it easier to turn ball over the bar or to go and meet the ball.

When practicing crosses:
1. The service must be realistic.
2. The coach must control the service of balls, otherwise the practice may degenerate into a pressure session with players unable to return to realistic positions due to lack of time.
3. The goalie and his defenders must be given the objective of gaining possession of the ball.
4. The coach must be prepared to demonstrate to the goalkeeper when bringing out a coaching point. (Even if in slow motion.)

Involvement off the line is undoubtedly the most difficult aspect of goalkeeping. The goalie should always try to get behind the line of flight. If he cannot pick the line of flight early, he should stay on his line.

A goalie should leave his line only for two reasons:
1. To cut down the angle of opportunity of the attacker.
2. To get the ball.

Once the goalie decides to go out, he must do so quickly. He must let his defenders know what he is going to do. He should not go out if his chances are not better than the other players.

When a goalie sees a cross coming, he must consider:
1. The distance of the ball from the goal. Will he be the best man to deal with that particular situation?
2. The path of the ball. Are there other players in the way?

The goalie must have superior understanding with his back players. They must always cover for each other. For example: if the ball is crossed inside his fullbacks, he must collect it, and again he must tell them that he is coming. The goalie should try to get the crosses at the highest possible point, and always try to go forward to meet the ball, and when he does come out, the back players should always cover the goal.

1) Crosses from both sides.

Practice for 12 players. X and Y take the ball to either side of the goal near the corner and cross for A and B to score. The keeper must make up his mind late and quickly to either come out to gather the ball, or to stay on the line and make a save. When he does either of these, he must now find X and Y with his throws with C trying to intercept. Now X and Y take the ball to the other goal and cross as before and repeat.

2) Reactions.

In the penalty area, play 3 vs. 3 or 4 vs. 4, or whatever the coach desires. Server sends ball across. Keeper and defenders must react to the situation. Important coaching points 1. Starting position of the keeper. 2. Importance of early (correct) decisions. 3. Clear, concise, confident calling. 4. Defenders reactions when goalie goes out. 5. The techniques in making contact with the ball.

GOALKEEPING EXERCISES

1) Jogging laterally crossing legs w/out ball.

2) jogging backward turning and sprinting without ball.

3) jogging forward kicking heels up w/out ball.

4) jogging forward bringing knee up high w/out ball.

5) jogging forward doing forward rolls w/out ball.

6) jogging forward doing quick deep knee bend w/out ball.

7) jogging forward and changing speed w/out ball.

8) jogging backward and doing backward rolls w/out ball.

9) jogging forward doing forward rolls with ball.

10) hopping while bouncing ball w/2 hands waist high.

60

11) hopping while bouncing ball around body exchanging hands.

12) holding ball at head high, dropping it and catching at shoe tops.

13) tossing ball between legs over shoulder, turning, jumping, and catching it.

14) rolling ball on ground around spread legs while standing.

16) rolling ball on ground from side to side under chest while lying on stomach.

15) rolling ball on ground around outstretched legs while sitting.

17) receiving ball tossed at various directions while standing.

18) receiving ball on both sides while sitting.

19) receiving ball on both sides while crouched, diving to save.

20) receiving ball on both sides while kneeling.

21) receiving ball on both sides while standing. Diving.

22) Ball rolled through the legs from front, turning and diving on it.

23) receiving ball on one side while pushing off w/lower leg and diving.

24) 2 GK balls, close range, one tosses and one rolls ball ... at each other.

25) 2 GK 2 balls, close range. Both bouncing balls at each other.

26) 2 GK 1 ball. Close range. Kicking & throwing ball at each other.

27) Punting and catching against a kickboard using both feet.

28) 2 GK 1 ball. Distance punting ball to each other.

29) receiving high ball in front of a goal, punting ball quickly.

30) kicking goal kick off ground.

31) Ball tossed from close quarters to GK in front of goal.

32) Tapping a crossed ball over goal.

33) Punching away from goal a crossed ball.

34) GK vs. attacker approaching the goal w/ball.

35) Leaving goal to receive high crossed ball.

36) Receiving shots from outer edge of penalty area.

37) Using feet to stop shots at goal.

GAMES

The GAMES portion of the practice should be a natural extension of the SKILL portion, so that there is a possibility of "transfer" of techniques into game situations. In general, rules should be kept to a minimum. The important thing is the "spirit of the game."

Small Side Scrimmage Game

Basic rules:
1. Divide your players into two teams of different colors, 6 to 8 to a side, of equal ability (as near as possible).
2. Playing field is approx. 30 x 60 yds. with goals 12 yds. wide made of cones or flags. Mark a goal area in a semi-circle of 20 ft. radius using t-shirts or any suitable material.
3. No off sides.
4. Normal throw-ins can be taken, or the ball can be side-footed or rolled along the ground into play.
5. The game commences by the ball being thrown out by one of the goal-keepers. When a goal is scored, the game re-commences in the same way.
6. A ball played over the goal line, by an attacker or defender, is returned to play by the goalkeeper rolling it with an under-arm action.
7. Only the defending goalkeeper is allowed inside his own goal area, and he may handle the ball only in this area.
   Penalty for infringement:
   a) By the defense — a Penalty Kick.
   b) By the attacking team — a Free-Kick at the point of entry into the circle.
8. All other infringements — Indirect Free Kick.
9. A goal can be scored from anywhere outside the goal area.
10. Charging is forbidden.
11. The game is controlled by a referee. May be the coach or one of the players. Allow no arguing with the referee's calls.

Conditioned Games

The Small Side Scrimmage Game can also be "conditioned" so that the attention of the players is focused on a particular aspect of the game. Only one condition should be used at a time and for only about five minutes.

The conditions imposed can be related to a particular skill being taught. Here are some examples:

Passing
1. The ball must not go above waist height. This insures that the ball is played with the feet.
2. A player can only touch the ball twice before passing it. This condition prevents a player from holding on to the ball too long and will cause his teammates to run into open space to receive a pass.
3. The ball must be passed with the inside of the foot.
4. The ball must be passed with the outside of the foot.

5. No pass should be more than 5 yds. This cuts out long, aimless passes.

Penalty for infringement of any of the above: Indirect Free Kick.

Dribbling and Challenging
1. The player in possession must "take on" an opponent, trying to beat him before passing or shooting. This condition will obviously encourage challenging.

Penalty: Indirect Free Kick.

Heading
1. A goal can only be scored with a header.
2. All returns to the field must be made with a header — including corners and goal kicks.

Penalty for infringement: Indirect Free Kick.

Basic Tactics
1. A player must never stand still after he has passed the ball.
2. The passer of the ball must call "HOLD" or "PASS" to the receiver.

Penalty for infringement: Indirect Free Kick.

Other Games

There are numerous games that include techniques from soccer or other games that can be played to increase the general level of skill and tactical answers. Here are a few:

1. **Soccer Baseball.**
   Two teams of equal numbers. Home plate is in front of the goal. Bases are placed according to the age of the players. Pitcher passes or rolls the ball to the batter who kicks the ball (practice instep kicking) to the outfield and proceeds around the bases as in baseball.

   Batter tries to run all the bases before the outfielders score into the goal (home plate). Outfielders can get the runner out only by scoring a goal. May use a goalkeeper. Three outs and change sides.

2. **Soccer Tennis.**
   The net can be a piece of string or rope about three or four feet high, between two posts, or you can play four vs. four on a regular tennis court. The rules can be made to suit the skill level of the players. In its simplest form, the ball is allowed to bounce once before it is returned with any part of the body except the hands. It can, however, be modified to allow two or three contacts on one side with or without a bounce between each contact. The game is started with an underhand throw from the baseline and can be played by any of the receiving team.

3. **Heading Tennis.**
   This game is played with a team of four to six using the same size court, but raising the (net) to four or six feet. Only headers can be used. Again, the rules can be made to suit the ability of the players. The ball can be returned first time or it can be headed two or three times before returned. A light plastic ball can be used for younger players.

4. **Extra Player Games.**

In these games, an extra player joins whichever side has possession of the ball. Thus, in a small side scrimmage game, the team in possession loses his extra player(s) to the other side as soon as they are successfully challenged. With less skillful players, there can be as many as three extra players. This game helps convince the players of the importance of good passing and control to retain possession of the ball.

5. **Uneven Team Games.**

Sides of uneven size play each other but have different targets. For example, in a four vs. two game, the four might be asked either: (a) to attack a smaller goal or (b) to score in a more difficult way, e.g. control the ball over their opponents' goal line while their opponents score normally. This game again stresses the importance of possession and the importance of the outnumbered team containing or jockeying its opponents.

INDIVIDUAL SKILL DEVELOPMENT PROGRAM

This program can be given to the individual to use at home to continue his skill development. A daily program like this will improve your techniques tremendously. You will find that constant repetition is the key to improving your skills.

Allow one minute for each of the following exercises:

1. **Head juggling.**
2. **Dribbling** — Practice tight ball control. (Keep ball close).
3. **Thigh juggling.**
4. **Dribbling** — Practice changing directions quickly.
5. **Instep juggling.**
6. **Dribbling** — Practice changing speeds — start slowly and accelerate for a distance of 10 yards, and then go slowly again.
7. **Combined juggling** — Combine head, thigh and instep juggling.
8. **Dribbling** — Combine change of direction and speed.

After doing each of the above exercises for one minute, start over and repeat each exercise for one minute more.

Now spend 10 minutes working on ball control. Throw or kick ball against a wall. Control ball on return and repeat. If you have a partner, have him throw or kick the ball to you.

Work 15 minutes on all types of passing. Set up targets at 10 yard, 20 yard, and 30 yard distances. (Chairs, shirts, rocks, etc. can be used as targets.) Start passing stationary balls to the targets, and then dribble to a spot and pass while moving. Use both your left and right feet to pass.

Work 10 minutes on heading. Head the ball against a wall. Strive to keep it in motion; count the number of repetitions and try to improve every day. Stand close to wall while heading.

Work 10 minutes on dribbling. Set up an obstacle course using trees, shirts, cones, etc. and dribble around them. Strive for top speed and ball control while dribbling.

BASIC TEAM TACTICS

The word TACTICS is one of the most misunderstood words relating to soccer. Some people will read a book which delves into such tactical maneuvers as "cross over plays," "overlapping half or fullbacks," "diagonal runs" and on and on. They mistakenly want to try this with youth teams. Even some of the best college teams cannot execute such tactics.

A simple give and go pass is a tactic. A three on one is a tactic. Proper defensive coverage falls into the area of tactics. Soccer is a simple game. Keep it that way. Let your team develop through the fundamentals and expand your use of tactical things as both you and they develop.

The Principles of Attack

As you might relate it to your team.

Our attack starts at the moment when any player on our team gets the ball, e.g. the goalkeeper or any other player for the kick-off, free-kick, throw-in, corner-ball, or the first pass.

Our first pass is as important as our last pass and must be well prepared, because our attack begins with the first pass and has to be finished by the last pass and final goal shot.

A successful attack will develop step-by-step according to the following pattern:

1. Running into open space   MOBILITY
2. Playing without the ball   MOBILITY
3. Combination of play   DEPTH, WIDTH, PENETRATION
4. Dribbling   IMPROVISATION
5. Goal Shot   FINISHING

1. **Running into open space.**
There are "dead" spaces and open spaces during play. In order to keep the ball for our team, every player has to run out of the "dead" spaces into the open spaces. Mobility keeps the ball moving. Nobody is faster than the ball and nobody has better endurance. "Use the ball" is still the best advice for every attack.

If you are trying to improve your peripheric sight, and looking around and thinking in advance, you will find the open space and will be prepared for every necessary action.

2. **Playing Without The Ball.**
Running free into open space is, of course, playing without the ball. But, in general, the player who runs free wants to receive the ball. Therefore, we differentiate between these two actions. Obviously every player who is running to open space cannot get the ball, but a smart player knows many tricky ways to drag an opponent away and to open the space for a teammate. This is playing without the ball.

3. **Combination Play.**
   Running free into open space and playing without the ball is the preparation of combination play. According to the organization of our opponents defense, there are two different ways we can attack. 1. If our opponents are well prepared to stop our attack, we will have to use the midfield and keep the ball until we find open spaces for successful through-passes. 2. If our opponents' defense is less well organized, we shall use a fast counterattack to beat them.

4. **Dribbling. (Improvisation)**
   Our match practice has been teaching us three kinds of dribbling. 1. To hold the ball until a teammate is in a free position to receive a pass. 2. To dribble, beat your opponent, and drag your teammates' opponent along, thus playing your teammate free. 3. To beat one or two opponents and score, or let a teammate score.

5. **Goal Shot**
   Everything we did so far is nothing without finishing. There is no substitute for goals.

Principles of Defense

As you may relate it to your team.

Our defense is the necessary stronghold from which our attack can be started. If we are weak in defense, we obviously cannot stop our opponent; but furthermore, we cannot control the pace of the game, and we cannot launch successful attacks.

Our defense starts at the moment when any player on our team has lost the ball. A well organized defense is developing step-by-step in the following pattern:

1. Immediate Chase	DELAY
2. Fall Back	
3. Man To Man	CONCENTRATION-BALANCE
4. Zone Defense	
5. Attack Man and Ball	CONTROL RESTRAINT

1. **Immediate Chase.**
   It is human nature that a player who has lost the ball wants to take a break, but players who rest on defense or attack are no longer useful teammates. The valuable team player has to do his job, both on attack and defense, without a break. That means, he must chase immediately after his opponent. Maybe you get the ball back; maybe you will make your opponent nervous, and the result is a mispass; but in any case, you engage him in a dual and your team wins time.

2. **Fall Back**
   After our team has lost the ball, our forwards are our first defenders. They have to chase immediately after their opponents.

   The next defenders are our midfielders (halfbacks). Their job is to delay the opposite attack. They are moving back as far as shooting distance to allure the opponents to waste time in the midfield. At this time, the defense gets organized for the coming battle.

3. **Man To Man**

    In shooting distance, man to man marking and organized zone defense are prepared. The closer the ball comes to your man, the tighter you must mark him. The farther the ball is away, the more distance is allowed between yourself and your opponent.

    A back player has to control the man and the ball. He has to stay between his man and the goal, and he must be sure that all passes towards his opponent are running in front of him and not into open space behind his back.

    If possible, a back player tries to get the ball before his opponent; but at least he attacks the forward at the moment of ball contact. If both actions are impossible, the back player has to show all his skill and class to stop the forward with the ball.

    Summary of the position of back players:

MATCH	1.	Defensive player must always watch over opponent and ball.
STAY	2.	Always stay between man and goal (Line up with the ball and goal).
	3.	Every pass to your man has to run in front of you. (Not into spaces behind you — blind side).
FIRST AIM	4.	If there is a pass to your man, stay back and try to intercept.
SECOND AIM	5.	Tackle as soon as he gets it, at his weakest moment. Don't act careless.
THIRD AIM	6.	Challenge him with your best. Force him to sideline.

4. **Zone Defense.**

    In general, a well organized defense marks man to man on ball-side of the field, and covers the other side. The combination of man to man marking and covering is the best way to organize a defense effectively. That means that every defender controls, at all times, both the man and the ball, and is prepared to cover for his teammate.

    Tight man to man marking is sometimes very important but not always very difficult. Clever zone defense needs more ability, experience and training.

    The organized defense within shooting distance around the goal, concentrated and well balanced, is hard to beat.

5. **Attack Man and Ball.**

    The best back players are not only robust and tough, but also clever and masters of fainting. If necessary, they attack resolutely and vigorously. In other situations, they prepare traps for the forwards and snatch the ball away, sometimes without body contact. Good defenders will never attack blandly. They are masters of what we call timing, control and restraint.

    As soon as our defenders have the ball, they start immediately for a promising counter attack.

Techniques

ball control
and trapping

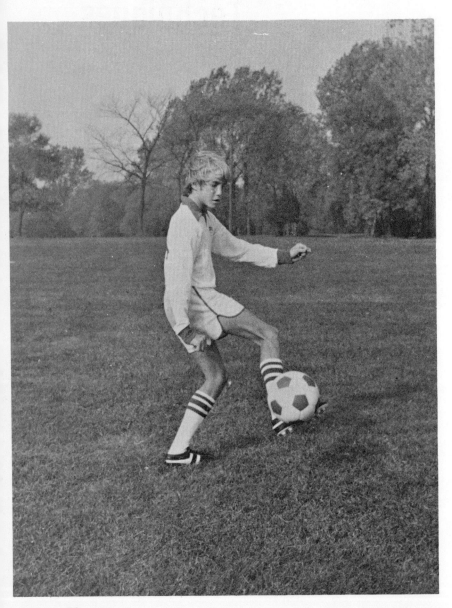

Ball Control

To play soccer a player first must learn to handle a soccer ball. Once he develops a reasonable proficiency with the ball, he must convert this technique into skill, which is the ability to implement technique under the physical and mental pressure of match play.

In developing soccer skills it is best to work first on pure technique, then hold practice under match-like conditions including a mild form of pressure from one or more opponents, and finally hold practice under match conditions including the same amount of pressure from opponents as is encountered in an actual match.

The ability to control a soccer ball is essential to playing the game. This includes not only stopping a ball or "trapping" it, but also receiving a ball without totally stopping it and playing it immediately after gaining control. Whenever possible a player should position himself in line with the direct flight of the ball and attempt to bring it under control with the largest possible body surface in order to minimize the chances of error.

The soccer player must be able to control a ball coming from any angle and at any speed. He must develop confidence in his technical ability to control balls quickly under all of the pressures of match play.

In the past, players were generally afforded much more time to play the ball than they are today. Players used to receive the ball, control it, look around to evaluate the situation and then play it. Today, however, opponents pressure players far more than ever before, and thus the amount of time that a player has to control a received ball has been decreased tremendously. Since the space and time that a player has to bring a ball under his control today is very limited, players must not only bring the ball under their control very quickly, but they must also know what they plan to do with the ball before they receive it.

After receiving and bringing the ball under his control, a player really has only one of three options: (1) he can pass the ball, (2) he can shoot the ball or (3) he can dribble it. The amount of time he has to do any of these actions directly depends on how quickly and efficiently he controls the ball immediately after receiving it.

Trapping Balls on the Ground

Sole of Foot

Face the oncoming ball with your eyes on the ball. Hold the sole of the trapping foot obliquely and wedge the ball between

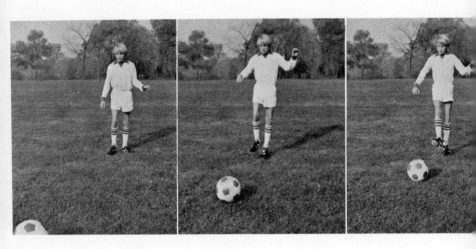

1. FACE BALL. KEEP EYES ON BALL.
2. HOLD SOLE OF FOOT OBLIQUELY, KEEP HEEL CLOSE TO GROUND. KNEE IS BENT.

the ground and the sole. Keep the heel close to the ground as the ball makes contact. The trapping foot should recoil slightly on contact.

This method of controlling a ball is helpful for beginning players since the technique is a relatively simple one to master. However, more advanced players will generally utilize other techniques, such as using the inside or outside of the foot, for controlling balls on the ground.

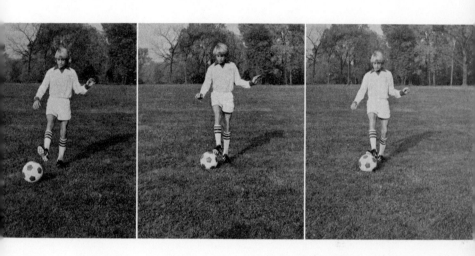

3. WEDGE BALL BETWEEN GROUND AND SOLE OF FOOT.

Inside of Foot

This trap is used quite extensively. With practice a player can trap and pass with one movement.

Beginning players must keep in mind that the foot should not be lifted so high that the ball passes under it, and to withdraw the foot on contact to avoid rebounding the ball.

Outside of Foot

This technique is used when the ball approaches from the side.

The main points to keep in mind when using this technique are the same as for controlling the ball with the inside of the foot — cushion the ball on contact and don't lift your foot too high.

1. FACE BALL. KEEP EYES ON BALL.
2. BEND KNEE AND POINT TOE OUTWARD.
3. CONTACT BALL IN FRONT OF BODY. TRAP BALL BETWEEN GROUND AND INSIDE OF FOOT.
4. WITHDRAW FOOT SLIGHTLY ON CONTACT TO AVOID REBOUND.

1. KEEP EYES ON BALL.
2. BEND KNEE CLOSER TO BALL AND POINT TOE INWARD.
3. MEET BALL AWAY FROM BODY WITH OUTSIDE OF FOOT.
4. WITHDRAW FOOT SLIGHTLY ON CONTACT TO AVOID REBOUND.

Trapping Balls in the Air

Inside of Foot

Keep your eyes on the ball and your body in balance. Raise your foot off the ground with the inside pointing toward the descending ball. Speed is taken off the ball by recoiling your foot on contact.

1. FACE BALL. KEEP EYES ON BALL.

Instep

This trap requires quick reflexes and often proves difficult to perform well.

Shift weight to non-trapping leg, bending slightly at the knee. Raise trapping leg as far as possible from the hip while bending the knee. Keep foot flexible and contact the ball with the full instep.

Drop your foot rapidly at first, then slow your descent as the foot and ball near the ground. This action takes the speed off

2. MAINTAIN PROPER BODY BALANCE BY EXTENDING ARMS.

3. RAISE FOOT OFF GROUND AND POINT TOE OUTWARD, INSIDE OF FOOT POINTING TOWARD DESCENDING BALL.

4. CONTACT BALL IN FRONT OF BODY.

5. RECOIL FOOT ON CONTACT.

the ball permitting the ball to land on the ground within one or two feet of the kicking foot.

1. FACE BALL. KEEP EYES ON BALL.

2. SHIFT WEIGHT TO NON-TRAPPING LEG. BEND KNEE SLIGHTLY.

3. RAISE TRAPPING LEG, KNEE BENT, TOE POINTED TOWARD BALL.

4. CONTACT BALL WITH FULL INSTEP IN FRONT OF BODY.

5. DROP FOOT ON CONTACT THEN SLOW DESCENT AS FOOT AND BALL NEAR GROUND.

Outside of Foot

Shift your weight to the non-trapping leg, bending the knee slightly. Raise your other leg toward the ball with knee bent and toe pointed inward. Contact the ball in front of your body with the outside of your foot. Drop your foot rapidly on contact, then more slowly so foot and ball reach the ground together.

1. KEEP EYES ON BALL.

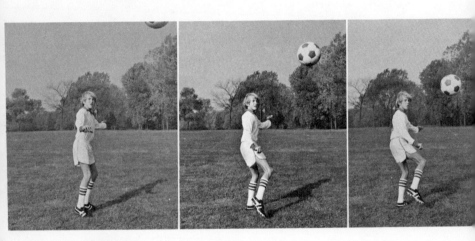

Thigh

Contact the ball at the midpoint of the thigh which is raised to a horizontal level. Recoil thigh at the moment of contact.

1. FACE BALL. KEEP EYES ON BALL.

2. SHIFT WEIGHT TO NON-TRAPPING LEG, BEND KNEE SLIGHTLY.
3. EXTEND TRAPPING LEG TOWARD BALL. BEND AT KNEE, POINT TOE INWARD.
4. CONTACT BALL WITH OUTSIDE OF FOOT.
5. DROP FOOT ON CONTACT AND BRING BALL TO GROUND.

2. LIFT LEG SO THIGH IS HORIZONTAL TO GROUND. CONTACT BALL AT MIDPOINT OF THIGH.
3. RECOIL THIGH ON CONTACT.

Chest

Always be careful to keep your arms away from the ball. With one foot kept in front of the other, arch the trunk of your body backward. Align chest with oncoming ball. Recoil on contact and let the ball fall to the ground.

1. FACE BALL. KEEP EYES ON BALL.
2. EXTEND ARMS FOR BALANCE.
3. ONE FOOT IN FRONT OF OTHER. ARCH TRUNK BACK.
4. CONTACT BALL AT TOP OF CHEST.
5. RECOIL ON CONTACT TO TAKE SPEED OFF BALL.

dribbling

Dribbling Techniques

Dribbling techniques enable a player to move the ball on the ground while jogging or running. It is used to get by an opponent while retaining possession of the ball.

1. KEEP BALL CLOSE TO FEET. KEEP EYES ON BALL.
2. KEEP WEIGHT ON NON-DRIBBLING FOOT.
3. USE WHATEVER PART OF FOOT IS MOST COMFORTABLE TO CONTACT BALL.
4. TAKE SHORT STRIDES WHILE DRIBBLING.
5. KEEP YOUR HEAD UP AS MUCH AS POSSIBLE TO DETERMINE WHERE YOU ARE GOING AND WHO IS AROUND YOU.

Dribbling While Being Marked

If an opponent challenges from the side, move the ball to the leg farther from the opponent.

This technique permits the dribbler to shield the ball from the defender with his body, but it obviously requires the player to master the technique of dribbling with both feet. Players who are unable to do this will invariably find themselves losing possession of the ball far too often.

1. **KEEP BALL CLOSE TO FEET.**
2. **CONTACT BALL ONLY WITH FOOT FARTHER FROM OPPONENT.**
3. **KEEP BODY BETWEEN OPPONENT AND BALL TO SHIELD BALL.**

Changing Direction

Keep the ball close to your feet and move it quickly. When the opponent closes in, pull the ball back with the sole of the foot on the far side of the opponent, turn quickly and continue dribbling in another direction.

1. KEEP BALL CLOSE TO FEET.
2. MOVE BALL QUICKLY.
3. WHEN OPPONENT IS CLOSE, PULL BALL BACK USING SOLE OF FOOT FARTHER FROM OPPONENT.
4. QUICKLY TURN AND DRIBBLE IN ANOTHER DIRECTION.

Step-Over Feint

Feinting while dribbling is a means of eluding an opponent. Learn to watch your opponents and teammates while maintaining control over the ball.

Step over the ball in the direction of the feint. If your opponent reacts, push the ball in the opposite direction.

1. KEEP BALL CLOSE TO FEET WHILE APPROACHING OPPONENT.
2. MOVE FOOT TO INSIDE AS IF BALL WILL BE PUSHED WITH OUTSIDE OF FOOT.
3. DO NOT CONTACT BALL — STEP OVER BALL WITH LONG STRIDE.
4. IF OPPONENT LEANS IN DIRECTION OF STEP-OVER, QUICKLY PUSH BALL IN OPPOSITE DIRECTION AND RUN BY OPPONENT.

Body Feint

If your opponent takes a long stride in the direction of your feint, push the ball between his legs and run around quickly to regain control of the ball.

The key factor to remember in successful feinting is not to make up your mind about what you will do with the ball until you see how the opponent reacts to the feint. Moreover, all feints must be convincing to the opponent or else he will not react to them in the desired manner.

1. KEEP BALL CLOSE TO FEET WHILE APPROACHING OPPONENT.

2. STEP IN ONE DIRECTION AND LEAN WITH HEAD AND SHOULDERS WITHOUT CONTACTING BALL.

3. IF OPPONENT LEANS IN DIRECTION OF FEINT, QUICKLY PUSH BALL IN OPPOSITE DIRECTION AND RUN BY OPPONENT.

4. IF OPPONENT TAKES LONG STRIDE IN DIRECTION OF FEINT, HE MAY SPREAD HIS LEGS WIDE ENOUGH TO ENABLE YOU TO PUSH BALL BETWEEN THEM.

5. RUN BY HIM TO REGAIN CONTROL OF BALL.

passing

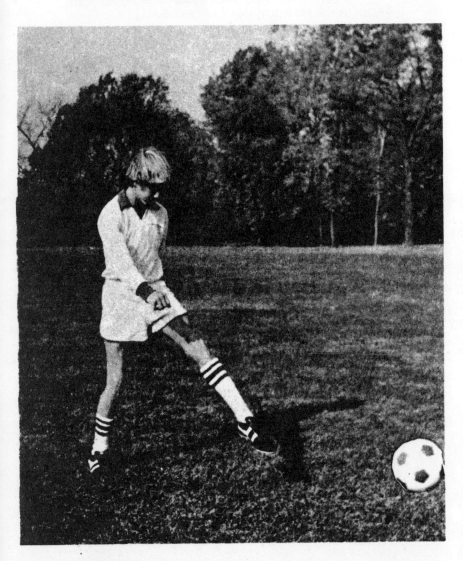

The members of a soccer team must play as a collective unit. To accomplish this, players must master the techniques of passing the ball to their teammates. Every time a player kicks the ball he should have a target in mind — either he passes to a teammate or he shoots on goal. Players should never simply kick the ball without having a target.

88

Kicking Techniques
Inside of Foot

With eyes on the ball, stride forward placing the non-kicking foot alongside and six inches away from the ball. At this point the non-kicking knee is bent slightly to allow weight to go forward on this foot. The kicking foot is turned outward. Notice as the kicking foot swings slightly backward it is lifted from the ground. Swing this foot forward forcefully using a push type action. Do not jab. Strike the ball at the midpoint for a low pass or kick. At this point the body will be leaning slightly backward at the hip. Continue with a good follow-through with the kicking leg.

1. KEEP EYES ON BALL.
2. PLACE NON-KICKING FOOT NEXT TO BALL AND ABOUT SIX INCHES AWAY.
3. WEIGHT IS ON NON-KICKING FOOT, KNEE SLIGHTLY BENT.

4. EXTEND ARMS FOR BALANCE.

5. KICKING FOOT IS BENT AT KNEE, TOE POINTED OUT.

6. CONTACT BALL WITH INSIDE OF FOOT. TO KEEP BALL ON GROUND CONTACT BALL AT MIDPOINT; TO LIFT CONTACT THROUGH LOWER HALF OF BALL.

7. FOLLOW THROUGH WITH KICKING LEG.

Outside of Foot

Techniques for kicking with the outside of your foot are the same as for using the inside of your foot, except that the toe of the kicking leg is pointed inward and the ball is contacted with the outside of your foot.

1. TECHNIQUES ARE IDENTICAL TO PASSING WITH INSIDE OF FOOT, EXCEPT:

2. POINT TOE OF KICKING FOOT INWARD AND CONTACT BALL WITH OUTSIDE OF FOOT.

Heel

Since a player in possession of the ball usually faces the direction in which the ball will travel, the use of a heel pass will sometimes prove very effective at catching the defenders off-guard. However, since the player passing the ball in this manner is unable to see the man to whom he is passing the ball, verbal communication between teammates is essential. Players should not use this passing technique until they have practiced it often and have mastered it fairly well.

1. PLACE NON-KICKING FOOT BESIDE BALL, KNEE BENT. ADJUST FOR MOVEMENT IF BALL IS ROLLING FORWARD.

2. PASS KICKING FOOT OVER BALL.

3. BRING KICKING FOOT BACK TO CONTACT BALL WITH HEEL.

4. FOLLOW THROUGH FOR MAXIMUM POWER.

Instep

Inside of instep kicking is one of the most widely used kicks. This kick can be used for cross-field passes, centers, clearances, shots and swerved passes.

When kicking with the right foot, approach the ball from the left at an angle not more than 45 degrees from the direction which the ball will take. Place the non-kicking foot about even with the ball and nine to ten inches away. To loft the ball, place the non-kicking foot slightly behind the ball.

1. APPROACH BALL FROM SLIGHT ANGLE.

2. KEEP EYES ON BALL.

3. PLANT NON-KICKING FOOT NEXT TO BALL AND ABOUT TEN INCHES AWAY.

4. TRANSFER WEIGHT TO NON-KICKING FOOT AS KICKING FOOT IS BROUGHT BACK, BENT AT KNEE.

5. BEND NON-KICKING LEG SLIGHTLY, EXTEND ARMS FOR BALANCE.

With the left leg bent slightly at the knee and the body leaning away from the kicking foot, bend the upper portion of the body slightly forward. The upper body and the arms will help maintain balance. As you swing the kicking leg backward at the knee, turn the leg outward.

Bring the kicking leg forward with the knee slightly bent and the toe pointing outward and down. On the follow-through straighten the knee and swing the leg through, extending the kick from the hip.

6. **BEND UPPER BODY SLIGHTLY FORWARD AS KICKING FOOT IS BROUGHT BACK.**

7. **SWING KICKING FOOT DOWNWARD, TOE POINTED SLIGHTLY OUT AND DOWN.**

8. **CONTACT BALL WITH INSIDE OF INSTEP. TO KEEP BALL LOW MAKE CONTACT AT MIDPOINT OF BALL; TO LIFT, CONTACT LOWER MIDDLE HALF OF BALL.**

9. **KICKING LEG PERFORMS FULL FOLLOW-THROUGH TO ASSURE MAXIMUM POWER.**

Full Volley

The volley kick is used for low drives, lofts and for clearances when there isn't time to trap the ball. The ball is kicked while in the air before it touches the ground.

When a low drive is desired, contact the ball close to the ground. Keep your knee and body weight over the ball. Contact the ball on the backside.

1. **KEEP EYES ON BALL. FACE BALL.**
2. **WEIGHT IS ON NON-KICKING LEG. BRING KICKING FOOT BACK AS FOR INSTEP PASS.**
3. **EXTEND ARMS FOR BALANCE.**
4. **CONTACT BALL WITH INSTEP OF KICKING FOOT. MAKE CONTACT IN FRONT OF BODY AS BALL IS ABOUT KNEE HEIGHT.**
5. **FOLLOW THROUGH, BEND UPPER BODY SLIGHTLY FORWARD FOR BALANCE.**

Half-Volley

Contact the ball just after it hits the ground to kick it on the half-volley. Apply the same techniques as for the volley kick.

This technique is helpful when players must play a ball first-time and their run to the ball is too late for using the full volley. Proper timing of ball contact is essential.

1. **KEEP EYES ON BALL. FACE BALL.**
2. **WEIGHT IS ON NON-KICKING FOOT. BRING KICKING FOOT BACK AS FOR INSTEP PASS.**
3. **EXTEND ARMS FOR BALANCE.**
4. **CONTACT BALL WITH INSTEP OF KICKING FOOT. MAKE CONTACT IN FRONT OF BODY AS BALL BEGINS TO BOUNCE BACK UP OFF GROUND.**
5. **FOLLOW THROUGH.**

Outside-of-the-Heel Volley

This technique may be used if the ball approaches at waist height. The ball must be hit first-time.

1. KEEP EYES ON BALL.
2. AS BALL APPROACHES PLACE WEIGHT ON NON-KICKING LEG AND LEAN TO THAT SIDE.
3. BEND KICKING LEG AT KNEE, LIFT HEEL UP.
4. PIVOT ON BALL OF NON-KICKING FOOT. SWING KICKING LEG TOWARD BALL.
5. CONTACT BALL WITH OUTSIDE OF HEEL.
6. KEEP KICKING LEG BENT AT KNEE AT ALL TIMES AND SWING AS IF IT WERE A BAT WHILE PIVOTING ON NON-KICKING FOOT.

Bending the Ball

This technique is used to make the ball swerve during flight. Contact the ball with either the inside or the outside of the foot.

1. **KEEP EYES ON BALL.**
2. **PLACE NON-KICKING FOOT TO SIDE AND SLIGHTLY BEHIND BALL.**
3. **CONTACT IS MADE DIAGONALLY ACROSS BALL, NOT THROUGH IT, TO GIVE APPROPRIATE SPIN.**
4. **TO SWERVE BALL TO RIGHT, CONTACT BALL ON LEFT SIDE. TO SWERVE BALL RIGHT TO LEFT, CONTACT BALL ON RIGHT SIDE.**

heading

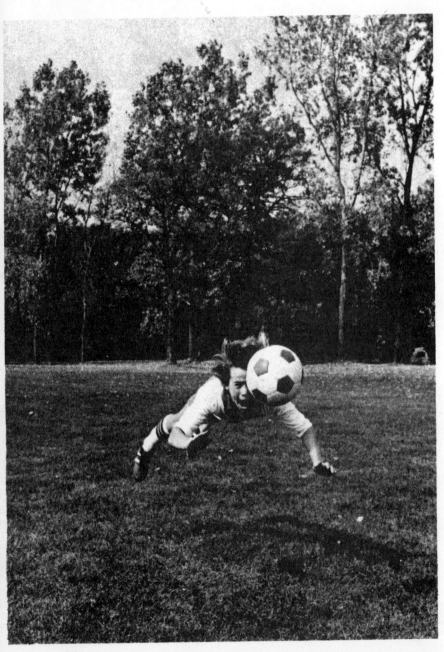

Heading Techniques

Whenever a ball is too high to be kicked and must be passed or shot it is contacted with the head. Generally players use their foreheads when heading a ball. This is a very hard part of the body which permits painless contact with the ball and, when proper heading techniques are used, can project the ball with considerable velocity and accuracy.

1. KEEP EYES ON BALL AT ALL TIMES.
2. AS BALL APPROACHES BEND KNEES SLIGHTLY. PLACE ONE FOOT BEHIND OTHER, ROCK BACK TRANSFERRING WEIGHT ONTO BACK LEG.
3. KEEP ARMS OUT FOR BALANCE.
4. ARCH UPPER BODY BACK, THEN SNAP UPPER BODY, NECK AND HEAD FORWARD AS BALL IS CONTACTED ON THE FOREHEAD.
5. TRANSFER WEIGHT TO FRONT LEG ON CONTACT.
6. DRIVE HEAD "THROUGH" BALL, FOLLOW THROUGH FOR MAXIMUM POWER.

Jump Heading

Both attacking and defending players must be able to head the ball while in the air. Especially in front of the goal, attackers will often be called on to jump and head in an attempt to score while defenders do the same in an attempt to get the ball from in front of their goal. Players who are poor ball headers will invariably find themselves at a great disadvantage on these occasions in every match.

Flick Heading (Backheading)

Backheading is often used by forwards to pass the ball when conventional heading becomes impractical because of an opponent's strong challenge.

Practice from a standing position at first, then from a jump. Bend knees and move head and trunk slightly backward. Contact the ball with the upper portion of your forehead. On contact, straighten knees and push forward from the hips.

1. KEEP EYES ON BALL.
2. JUMP UP AS BALL APPROACHES, ARCHING UPPER BODY BACK.
3. AT APEX OF JUMP, DRIVE UPPER BODY, NECK AND HEAD FORWARD TO CONTACT BALL WITH FOREHEAD.
4. EXTEND ARMS FOR BALANCE.

1. KEEP EYES ON BALL.
2. BEND KNEES SLIGHTLY, LEGS APART.
3. CONTACT BALL AT HAIRLINE OF FOREHEAD.
4. SNAP HEAD BACK ON CONTACT WITH BALL TO FLICK BALL.

Dive Heading

There are situations that occur during a match when diving and making contact with the head is the only way a player can strike the approaching ball. When teaching dive heading it is imperative to stress the proper technique of landing after contact with the ball is made. Otherwise, young players may be apprehensive of using this technique when it is needed.

1. KEEP EYES ON BALL.
2. DIVE FORWARD AS BALL APPROACHES.
3. FOREHEAD CONTACTS BALL AS BODY IS PARALLEL TO GROUND.
4. THRUST ARMS AND LEGS DOWN TO ABSORB SHOCK OF LANDING.

tackling

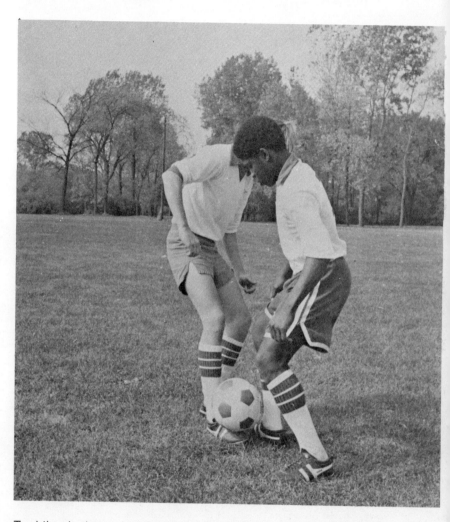

Tackling is the technique used to dispossess opponents of the ball in order to gain possession. When an opponent has the ball, the defender must first "jockey" or contain him until the opportunity arises to challenge for the ball.

Generally it is best to attempt a tackle either just as the opponent receives the ball and is still bringing it under control, or as the opponent pushes the ball forward and away from himself while dribbling.

Jockeying

Always jockey at an angle to the opponent to force him to dribble in the direction you wish him to go. Stay on the balls of your feet with your knees slightly bent so you can make quick changes of direction.

Occasionally feint as if you are challenging for the ball. This may unnerve the attacker and cause him to commit an error with the ball that will give you an opening for a tackle.

1. JOCKEY AT ANGLE TO OPPONENT.
2. STAY ON BALLS OF FEET WITH KNEES SLIGHTLY BENT.
3. KEEP EYES ON BALL.
4. FEINT OCCASIONALLY TO UNNERVE OPPONENT.

Sliding Tackle

This tackling technique is used as a last resort to dispossess an attacker of the ball, and should be avoided if there is any other means of winning the ball or dispossessing the opponent.

Approach your opponent from an oblique direction. Execute the tackle only when the opponent's inside leg is extended backward. Slide across and in front of your opponent to push or kick the ball out of play with the foot farther away from the opponent.

1. KEEP EYES ON BALL.
2. APPROACH OPPONENT FROM OBLIQUE DIRECTION.
3. SLIDE TOWARD BALL. CONTACT BALL WITH FOOT FARTHER AWAY FROM OPPONENT.
4. SLIDE INTO BALL AND KNOCK IT AWAY FROM DRIBBLING OPPONENT.

Block Tackle

Challenge for the ball as the attacking player pushes it forward and away from himself. Place the non-tackling foot next to the ball and transfer your weight to that leg. Bend your knees slightly and lean your upper body slightly forward, with the shoulder on the side of the tackling foot toward the opponent.

1. PLACE NON-TACKLING FOOT NEXT TO BALL AND SHIFT WEIGHT TO THAT LEG.

2. BEND KNEES SLIGHTLY AND LEAN UPPER BODY SLIGHTLY FORWARD, SHOULDER ON TACKLING SIDE TOWARD OPPONENT.

Make contact slightly below the midpoint of the ball with the inside of your foot. After stopping the progress of the ball attempt to win possession by lifting it over the opponent's foot or pushing it through between his legs.

Players must keep in mind that attempting to win possession of the ball through tackling is every bit as important as dispossessing the opponent of the ball.

3. **CONTACT BALL SLIGHTLY BELOW MIDPOINT WITH INSIDE OF FOOT.**

4. **AFTER STOPPING BALL, PUSH IT BETWEEN OPPONENT'S LEGS, OR LIFT IT OVER HIS FOOT.**

the throw-in

Every throw-in must be made with both feet on the ground behind the touchline. The ball must be thrown with equal force by both hands from behind and over the head.

Stationary Throw-In

Spread the fingers of both hands comfortably to grip the ball to the side and behind the ball. Keep your feet comfortably spread. Bring the ball behind your head with arms bent, then drive the trunk of your body forward, straightening your arms as the ball is brought forward over your head. Shift your weight to the balls of your feet. Release the ball once your hands are in front of your head. Follow through with your arms pointing toward the target for a throw.

1. GRIP BALL WITH BOTH HANDS TO SIDE AND BEHIND BALL, FINGERS COMFORTABLY SPREAD.

2. SPREAD FEET COMFORTABLY.

3. BRING BALL BEHIND HEAD WITH ARMS BENT.

4. DRIVE TRUNK FORWARD, STRAIGHTEN ARMS AS BALL IS BROUGHT FORWARD OVER HEAD. TRANSFER WEIGHT TO BALLS OF FEET.

5. RELEASE BALL WHEN HANDS ARE IN FRONT OF HEAD. FOLLOW THROUGH, ARMS POINTING TOWARD TARGET FOR THROW.

Running Throw-In

Techniques are essentially the same as for the stationary throw-in, except that a five- to six-yard run precedes the throw. Be sure that part of the back foot stays on the ground. Learn to "drag" the back foot.

1. GRIP BALL WITH BOTH HANDS TO SIDE AND BEHIND BALL, FINGERS COMFORTABLY SPREAD.

2. STRIDE FORWARD WITH ONE FOOT WHILE BRINGING BALL BEHIND HEAD WITH ARMS BENT AT ELBOWS. ARCH UPPER BODY BACK.

3. DRIVE TRUNK FORWARD. STRAIGHTEN ARMS AS BALL IS BROUGHT FORWARD OVER HEAD. SHIFT WEIGHT TO FRONT FOOT.

4. RELEASE BALL WHEN HANDS ARE IN FRONT OF HEAD. FOLLOW THROUGH WITH ARMS AND DRAG REAR FOOT FORWARD MAINTAINING CONTACT WITH GROUND.

shooting

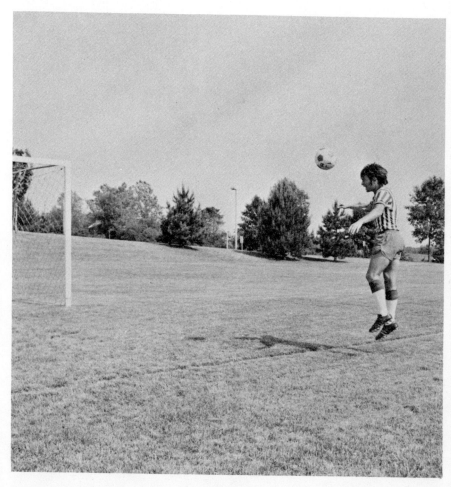

Shooting is nothing more than applying the techniques of passing to get the ball past the opposing goalkeeper and into the goal. Which technique to use at any one time must be decided by analyzing the game situation. Sometimes power can be more helpful than accuracy and vice versa. One main point to remember is that very rarely will a player shooting the ball be afforded much time by his opponents. As a result, all players must learn how to shoot as quickly as possible. Shooting balls first-time as they approach is a skill that all players must develop.

111

goalkeeping

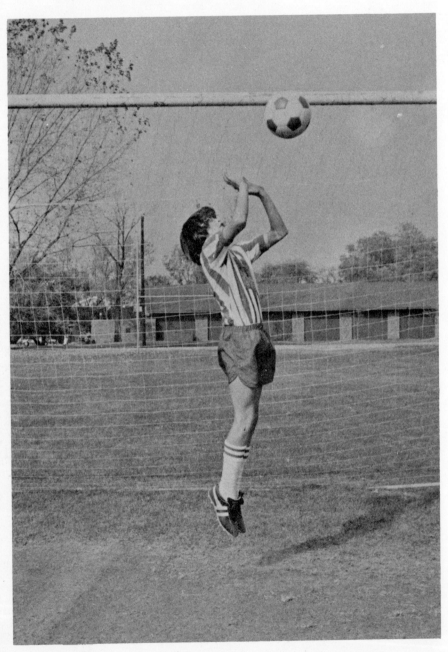

Defensive Goalkeeping

The goalkeeper is the only true specialist in the game of soccer. Unlike the field players, he is allowed to use his hands and thus has to master a unique set of techniques to perform in his position.

Ready Position

1. FEET COMFORTABLY SPREAD, KNEES JUST SLIGHTLY BENT.
2. BEND ARMS, HOLD OUT TO SIDE IN COMFORTABLE POSITION.
3. BEND UPPER BODY SLIGHTLY FORWARD, WEIGHT ON BALLS OF FEET, READY TO MOVE OR DIVE IN ANY DIRECTION.

Catching Ground Balls While Standing

When catching ground balls head on, face the approaching ball with feet together and legs straight. As the ball approaches, bend at the waist allowing your arms to drop with palms facing the ball and fingers spread. Hold your hands close together with elbows tucked in close to your body. Give with your hands as the ball makes contact. From this point bring the ball to your chest.

1. FACE BALL. KEEP EYES ON BALL.
2. PLACE FEET CLOSE TOGETHER. BEND DOWN AT WAIST.
3. EXTEND ARMS WITH HANDS CLOSE TOGETHER AND PALMS FACING BALL. ELBOWS ARE CLOSE TO BODY.
4. LET BALL COME INTO HANDS, THEN DRAW BALL CLOSE TO CHEST.

Catching Ground Balls
Half Kneeling

Kneel on one knee, placing it close to the heel of the other foot. Behind the hands, the thigh and shin seal off the ball from the goal. Arm and hand positions are the same as for catching ground balls while standing. This method of catching ground balls may be used as an alternative to the standing technique, and is especially helpful in catching ground balls that come from the side.

1. KEEP EYES ON BALL.
2. KNEEL ON ONE KNEE. PLACE KNEE CLOSE TO HEEL OF OTHER FOOT.
3. EXTEND ARMS WITH HANDS CLOSE TOGETHER, ELBOWS IN AND PALMS FACING BALL.
4. LET BALL COME INTO HANDS, THEN DRAW BALL IN CLOSE TO CHEST.

Catching Medium-High Balls

When catching balls at waist to shoulder height, face the ball with feet seven to nine inches apart and knees slightly bent. Project arms forward with palms up and elbows bent. As the ball makes contact with your arms and chest, the trunk should recoil slightly to reduce the shock of the ball's contact. Pull the ball into your body for protection.

Catching High Balls

Catching overhead balls depends a great deal on timing the approach and jump for the ball. As the ball approaches the goal, flex your knees in preparation for upward extension. Drive your body upward with full arm extension. Hold hands close together with palms facing the ball. Catch the ball with your fingers and draw it to a protective position.

1. FACE BALL. KEEP EYES ON BALL.

2. ARMS FORWARD, ELBOWS BENT, PALMS UP.

3. ALLOW BALL TO REACH CHEST AND CRADLE WITH ARMS AND HANDS.

4. KEEP ELBOWS CLOSE TOGETHER AFTER CATCHING BALL TO PREVENT DROPPING IT.

1. TAKE READY POSITION. KEEP EYES ON BALL.

2. JUMP UPWARD, EXTENDING ARMS TOWARD BALL WITH HANDS FAIRLY CLOSE TOGETHER, PALMS FACING BALL.

3. CATCH BALL WITH FINGERS AT APEX OF JUMP.

4. BRING ELBOWS IN AND CRADLE BALL AGAINST CHEST TO PROTECT BALL.

Two-Fisted Punching

If unable to catch the ball because of interference from an opponent, you may choose to punch the ball with one or both fists rather than attempt a catch. This strategy is especially helpful if the ball appears to be dropping under the crossbar.

Contact the ball at the height of your jump on the flat portion of your knuckles. Straighten your arms on contact and deflect the ball toward the touchline.

One-Fisted Punching

Using only one fist to punch the ball often permits the goalkeeper to make contact with those balls that he cannot reach with both fists. One-fisted punching will be less accurate than using both fists because of the smaller surface area used to make contact with the ball. Nevertheless it is a vital technique for goalkeepers to master and, with practice, can be used very effectively.

1. KEEP EYES ON BALL.

2. JUMP UPWARD WITH ARMS BENT AND NEAR CHEST.

3. AT APEX OF JUMP THRUST FISTS UPWARD, EXTENDING ARMS.

4. MAKE CONTACT WITH BALL ON FLAT PORTION OF FISTS, WITH FISTS TOGETHER.

5. PUNCH BALL OVER BAR OR CLEAR, DEPENDING ON SITUATION.

1. KEEP EYES ON BALL.

2. JUMP UPWARD, EXTENDING ONE ARM. KEEP PUNCHING ARM DOWN AND BENT.

3. AT APEX OF JUMP THRUST PUNCHING FIST UPWARD, EXTENDING ARM.

4. MAKE CONTACT WITH BALL ON FLAT PORTION OF FIST.

5. FOLLOW THROUGH.

Deflecting or Pushing High Balls over the Crossbar

Not every ball can be caught by the goalkeeper. Although the ball should be caught whenever possible, there are times that a save must be made by deflecting or pushing the ball over the crossbar. This situation most frequently occurs when the goalkeeper finds the ball too high for him to catch and yet still within contact range.

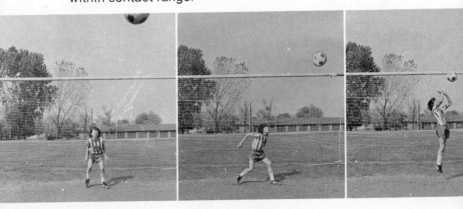

Lateral Diving Catch

Even when you are positioned properly, a ball still may be out of reach making a diving catch necessary. In diving you must catch the ball or clear the ball with a punch. When making either high- or low-diving catches apply similar techniques while adjusting for the height of the ball.

Drive your body toward the ball with your legs, achieving full body extension. Forearms and palms should face the approaching ball. Catch the ball with the fingers and bring it to your body. "Cradle" the ball between your arms and legs. After landing roll over to protect ball and body from the oncoming forwards.

1. KEEP EYES ON BALL.
2. JUMP UPWARD WITH ARMS EXTENDED BUT STILL BENT AT ELBOWS.
3. CONTACT BALL WITH FINGERS, EXTEND ARMS FULLY, AND PUSH BALL UP AND OVER CROSSBAR.

1. KEEP EYES ON BALL. ASSUME READY POSITION.
2. TAKE SHORT LATERAL STRIDE IN DIRECTION OF DIVE AND PUSH OFF FOOT CLOSER TO BALL.
3. KEEP ARMS BENT UNTIL LAST MOMENT.
4. FRONT OF BODY SHOULD FACE PLAYING FIELD DURING DIVING.
5. REACH OUT FOR BALL, EXTENDING ARMS, AND CATCH BALL WITH FINGERS.
6. LAND ON SIDE OF BODY. AVOID HITTING ELBOWS ON GROUND AND JARRING BALL.

Lateral Diving Punch

Whenever a ball is too far away to catch by diving the goal-keeper should punch it clear of the goal mouth with his fist. Whether to catch or punch the ball should be decided at the last moment when you can best judge whether catching it is possible.

1. **APPLY SAME TECHNIQUES AS FOR DIVING CATCH.**
2. **IF UNABLE TO CATCH BALL, PUNCH IT WITH EXTENDED ARM INSTEAD OF REACHING TO CATCH IT.**

Goalkeeper in Attack

Whenever a team wins possession of the ball it must immediately assume an attacking position. Whoever wins the ball must initiate the attack. When the goalkeeper catches the ball he must pass it on in such a way as to gain the deepest penetration into the defense of the opposition without sacrificing accuracy. Throwing or rolling the ball out to a teammate is safer than kicking it, since when kicking the goalkeeper sacrifices accuracy for deeper penetration. The main concern is not to lose the ball to the other team.

Rolling the Ball

Rolling the ball is a good clearing method because keeping the ball on the ground permits a teammate to gain control easily.

Always keep your eyes on the intended target. Step toward the target, release the ball on the ground and follow through.

1. **STRIDE IN DIRECTION THE BALL IS TO GO.**
2. **ROLL BALL TO TEAMMATE AS IF BOWLING.**
3. **FOLLOW THROUGH TO ACHIEVE MAXIMUM FORCE.**

Sling Throw

Spread your fingers to grasp the ball in the base of your palm.
Stride toward the target while bringing the ball behind your
body with extended arm and locked elbow. This enables the
arm to act as a catapult. Shift your weight to the rear leg and
arch back your upper body. Transfer your weight to the front
leg as your throwing arm and upper body thrust forward. Keep
your arm stiff. Follow through.

1. **HOLD BALL IN BASE OF PALM WITH FINGERS
   SPREAD.**

2. **STRIDE TOWARD TARGET WHILE BRINGING BALL
   BEHIND BODY WITH ARM EXTENDED AND ELBOW
   LOCKED.**

3. **TRANSFER WEIGHT TO REAR LEG. UPPER BODY IS
   ARCHED BACK.**

4. **TRANSFER WEIGHT TO FRONT LEG AS THROWING
   ARM AND UPPER BODY THRUST FORWARD.**

5. **ARM FOLLOWS THROUGH IN DIRECTION OF TARGET.**

Volley or Punt

This method is used to clear the ball for greatest distance. Always shield the ball from oncoming opponents. Extend your arms to drop the ball from about waist height. Keep your eyes on the ball. Thrust kicking foot forward as for a full volley kick contacting the ball on the instep. Follow through.

For half-volley or drop kick, the same techniques are used except that the ball is dropped to the ground and kicked on the bounce.

1. HOLD BALL IN FRONT OF BODY.

2. STRIDE FORWARD WITH NON-KICKING FOOT. SHIFT WEIGHT ONTO THAT FOOT WHILE BRINGING KICKING FOOT BACK AS FOR FULL VOLLEY KICK.

3. DROP BALL. KEEP EYES ON BALL.

4. BRING KICKING FOOT THROUGH AS FOR FULL VOLLEY KICK MAKING CONTACT WITH BALL ON INSTEP. FOLLOW THROUGH.

Diagram of Soccer Field

Detail of Corner Flag

5 FT.

132 FT.

60 FT.

54 FT.

18 FT.

CORNER FLAG

PENALTY AREA

30 FT.

TOUCH LINE

MAX.-360 FT. MIN.-300 FT.

60 FT.

HALF WAY LINE

TOUCH LINE

Penalty Kick Mark

30 FT.

54 FT.

18 FT.

36 FT.

GOAL AREA

24 FT.

CORNER FLAG

CORNER FLAG

MAX. 225 FT. MIN. 180 FT.

24 FT.

8 FT.

Detail of Goal Posts

basic tactics

The Goalkeeper

The primary task of the goalkeeper is to act as his team's last line of defense. He must prevent opposing players from scoring at his goal. He must have good hands to catch the ball, quick reflexes, courage and a sound working knowledge of the game in order to anticipate his opponents' attacks and to know when to come out of goal to attempt winning the ball. The goalkeeper controls the penalty area in front of him. His first duty is to intercept and win as many balls as he can in order to reduce the number of shots taken at his goal.

However, some shots are bound to be taken no matter how capable the goalkeeper. Therefore, the goalkeeper must so position himself for every shot that he can cover the maximum area of the goal by diving to make the save. Whenever the goalkeeper must leave a portion of the goal open, he should make certain he has all the space between himself and the nearer goal post covered, leaving open space by the far goal post which is a more difficult shot for the attacker.

Goalkeepers must learn to narrow the angle of shooting space. If an opposing player with the ball were coming at the goal and the goalkeeper stayed on the goal line, the opponent would enjoy the maximum shooting angle. However, if the goalkeeper moves toward the opponent the angle of space available for a goal attempt is reduced.

The Defenders

The role of the defenders is to prevent the other team from scoring goals. Thus, they must be adept primarily at marking men, jockeying and tackling, although in modern soccer all players should be able to perform the skills required by every position.

The Midfielders

The midfield position generally requires the greatest amount of endurance, since the midfielders' role is to link the team's defense and attack. More so than any of their teammates they are involved in defending their own goal as well as attacking the goal of the opposition. As a result they must master both defending and attacking skills.

Forwards

The primary task of forwards is attempting to score goals for their team. However, all players must help defend when opponents have the ball. It is small consolation to have scored three goals if your team concedes four and loses the game. Forwards must be adept dribblers as they will sometimes need to beat defenders in some one-on-one situations and must be good, accurate shooters in order to score goals.

Team Defense

There are several types of defensive strategy. Coaches can choose to use (1) zone defense, (2) man-for-man defense or (3) a combination of both.

In the *zone defense* each defender is assigned a given area of the field and is responsible for preventing successful attacking plays by the opposition in this area.

In *man-for-man defense* each defender is assigned one opponent to mark and contain regardless of where the opponent may go on the playing field. When using this kind of defense it is usually a good idea to position a free defender behind his teammates to provide them with cover and support.

A *combination of zone and man-for-man defense* incorporates some principles of both types. Generally the use of diagonal cover and support is used in this form of defensive structure.

When the ball is on the attacker's right wing, the left back marks the man with the ball while the other backs drop back in a diagonal line to provide support and cover. This prevents the player with the ball from being able to come in on goal uncontested in the event he gets by the left back, and prevents the ball from being passed behind the left back to another attacker to beat the entire defense.

The following basic principles are essential for all defensive play:

1. *Delay your opponents' attack* when your team first loses possession of the ball to permit the defense to regroup and organize.

2. Provide *support* for one another as is done, for instance, in diagonal covering.

3. As the ball approaches the goal *concentrate the defense in front of the goal,* thus limiting the space available for goal attempts.

4. *Maintain defensive balance.* Never position all the defenders on one side of the field at the same time — the opponents may manage to get the ball to the other side.

5. *Pressure the attacking player* in possession of the ball. Force him to make errors by limiting the time and space he has to play the ball.

6. *Control yourself.* Do not make rash commitments that lead you away from a good defensive position or challenge for the ball during an inopportune moment.

Team Attack

The following basic principles are essential for all offensive play:

1. It is most important, of course, to *maintain possession of the ball.* You cannot score goals unless you have the ball and while you retain it the other team cannot score.

2. Always *support the player who has the ball.* Ideally he should always have two or three teammates within 15 yards to whom he can pass the ball if necessary.

3. Maintain as much *width* as possible in your attack. Try to use the entire width of the field when possible.

4. Every pass should *penetrate as deeply as possible* into the defense of the opposition without undue risk of losing possession.

5. Attacking players should *move about and interchange positions* frequently to find space for passing opportunities and to make the opponents' task of defending against them more difficult.

6. Soccer is a quick reaction game and all players should be encouraged to *improvise* according to the momentary game situation.

7. Scoring goals often requires quickness and first-time shooting. To win the game you must *finish your attacks with shots on goal.*

Systems
of Play

WM Formation

One of the most basic offensive and defensive patterns for beginners is the *WM formation.* The three fullbacks and the wing halfbacks form the *M;* the *W* is formed by the insides, wingers and center forward. This formation covers the field well and gives depth to the offense and defense.

In this formation the defensive coverage is comprised of fullbacks on the wingers, wing halfbacks covering the opposing inside man and the center half or center fullback covering the center forward.

WM FORMATION

Inverted W Formation

Variations of this offensive pattern constitute the *Inverted W formation* which retains the three-back defense. In this formation, the center forward assumes a position in line with the wingers. If the defense challenges with fullbacks on the wingers, halfbacks on the inside men and the center half covering the center forward, the opposition is then in a defense which it is not accustomed to playing. It means the center half moves farther into the midfield and cannot play his "stopper" position. The fullbacks are pulled out of their normal positions and moved farther upfield to challenge the wingers. The halfbacks are now playing a "stopper role" because the opposing inside men are playing a double center forward position. All of this creates problems for the opposing defense. Intelligent forwards sometimes can capitalize on this situation before the other team can adjust.

INVERTED W FORMATION

4-2-4 Formation

The *4-2-4 formation* became quite popular during the 1950s. For this formation use two midfield players who are quite gifted and who have a great deal of stamina since they must attempt to control the entire middle of the field. The wing forwards should come deep into their defense to help when their team is defending, and the wing backs should move forward in support of the attack.

4-2-4 FORMATION

4-2-4 Formation Using a Sweeper Back

A variation of a normal 4-2-4 formation is to use a sweeper back and only three men in the defensive back line. This provides the defense with additional support and cover and would also permit the use of a man-for-man defense.

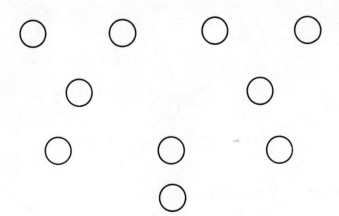

4-2-4 FORMATION USING A SWEEPER BACK

4-3-3 and 3-3-4 Formations

These two variations of the 4-2-4 are formed from that formation by moving one man to midfield from the four backs or the
four forwards, depending on whether the team needs defensive or offensive strength.

4-3-3 FORMATION

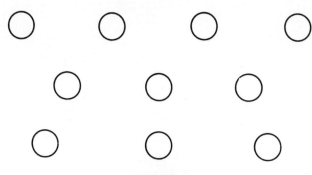

3-3-4 FORMATION

Team Play

In selecting a system, the formation must be compatible with the players. A coach should never attempt to force a particular formation on his players. Also, a formation is not rigidly held throughout the game. It is only a framework through which different plays are worked. After each play has terminated, the players move back into formation.

Soccer is played with the men positioned in a series of interlocking triangles which add depth to both the offense and defense. This means that forwards and defense men must not attack or defend on a "flat front." In a situation where three backs stand in a straight line across the field, none of the three can cover the space behind each of the other players on a through pass. Furthermore, four forwards attacking in a straight line across the field limit the passing possibilities.

As in any team game the more that the players practice together, the better the system works. Each man must completely understand his role in the formation. Also, he must have a knowledge of the duties of the men around him. Only then can he be expected to function effectively as a member of the team.

Rules

Playing Rules

LAWS OF THE GAME

The definitive laws of the game of soccer are those of F.I.F.A., the "Federation International de Football Association", or, in English: the International Federal of Association Football. These laws apply all over the world and provide a standard which governs international competition.

The North American Soccer League, the American Soccer League, Soccer Association For Youth, the United United States Soccer Federation, the National Collegiate Athletic Association and the Federation of State High School Associations all have their own set of laws, or rules, which basically conform to the F.I.F.A. laws, but which also have variations peculiar to that particular organization.

Various youth soccer programs also have made further changes to allow for problems specific to young players.

The F.I.F.A. laws of the game shall apply to play, except as may be amended in this book which appear in bold type. The laws, as listed herein, are intended to change the nature of the game as little as possible, and are primarily directed toward creating a safer game for the participants, and providing means for all players to participate.

Law One — THE FIELD OF PLAY

The field of play and appurtenances shall be as shown on the diagram.

1. **Dimensions**

    Recommended field sizes are as follows:

PASSERS:	60 x 80 yards
WINGS:	60 x 90 yards
STRIKERS:	60 x 100 yards
KICKERS:	65 x 110 yards
MINORS AND SENIORS:	70 x 110 yards

    Wherever possible, the size of the field should be related to the age division using it.

2. Marking
    The field shall be marked with distinctive lines, not more than 5 inches in width. The longer lines shall be called the touchlines, and the shorters lines the goal-lines. (Marking must be with marble dust or latex paint, or some material which is not injurious to eyes or skin.)

    A halfway line shall be marked across the field of play. From the midpoint of this line, a ten-yard radius circle shall be marked.

    A flag on a post at least 5 feet high will be placed at each corner of the field. Similar flags may be used to mark midfield, but must be at least one yard outside of the touchlines.

3. The Goal Area
    The goal area is marked by lines perpendicular to the goal line six yards into the field, and joined by a line parallel to the goal line.

4. The Penalty Area
    The penalty area is marked by lines perpendicular to the goal line 18 yards from each goal-post, extending 18 yards into the field, and joined by a line parallel to the goal line. A penalty-kick mark shall be made 12 yards from the goal line, opposite the center of the goal. From the penalty-kick mark, an arc of radius 10 yards shall be drawn outside the penalty area.

5. The Corner Area
    A quarter circle, or radius 1 yard, shall be drawn inside the four corners of the field.

6. The Goals
    The goals are placed at the midpoint of each goal line, with each upright the same distance from the corner flag, and 24 feet apart (inside measurement), joined by a crossbar 8 feet from the ground (lower edge). Uprights and crossbar should have the same width. Goal nets shall be attached to the posts and crossbar and fastened to the ground in such a manner as to not interfere with the goalie.

NOTES:

1. All markings are part of the areas they enclose.

2. Goals should be painted white.

3. Penalty areas, goal areas, and 10-yard circles are not to be reduced in size on smaller fields, nor is the goal size to be reduced from 8-foot by 24-foot inside measurements.

4. If a crossbar becomes damaged and falls, or is in danger of falling, it must be removed. League games may continue, with the approval of both coaches, with the referee's judgement determining whether any particular shot would have been under the crossbar, had one been there. However, tournament games will require that a solid crossbar be in place. Damage to the crossbar must be repaired, or the game moved to another field.

5. If the field is not adequately lined, the game will proceed, according to the best of the referees' ability to determine the position of the lines. If there are no nets on the goals, the game will proceed to the best of the referee's judgment..

6. A referee may refuse to start a game, or may stop it once play has started, if in the referee's judgment, the condition of the ground is such as to endanger the players. In the event of an electrical storm, play must be stopped until the danger has passed. If a game has been stopped after at least one-half has been played, and it cannot be re-started, it shall be considered an official game. If less than one-half has been played, it must be re-scheduled in its entirety.

Law Two — THE BALL

The ball shall be spherical; the outer casing shall be of leather or other approved material. No material shall be used which might be dangerous to the players.

Passers (6,7) will use a No. 3 Ball, Wings (8, 9) and Strikers (10,11) will use a No. 4 Ball. Kickers, Minors and Seniors (12-18) will use a No. 5 Ball.

The game ball will not be changed during the course of the game without the approval of the referees.

NOTES:

1. If the ball becomes deflated during play the game shall be stopped and re-started by dropping a new ball where the deflated ball was last played, but never inside the penalty area. (See "drop ball", Law Eight). If it is found to be deflated during a stoppage of the game it will be replaced and the game re-started normally.

Law Three — PLAYERS AND SUBSTITUTIONS

A game will be played by two teams, each consisting of not more than eleven nor less than seven players, one of whom shall be the Goalkeeper. Each team shall designate one player as a Captain. If he or she leaves the game, another Captain must be designated. The active Captain is the only player permitted to discuss a rule interpretation with the referees.

Before all players on a team have completed playing their team required quarters (Passers = 2, Others = 1), a team may substitute only for an injured or cautioned member of that team, and between quarters. Partial quarters played do not count toward fulfillment of personal required playing time, but do count toward the team's required playing time as it pertains to free substitutions. An ejected player may not be replaced; the team will play short for the remainder of the game. A player who was present at the start of the game and enters the game for the first time as a substitute for an injured or cautioned player must play another entire quarter (Passers = 2 quarters) before the team achieves free substitution status.

During the progress of the game, the referees must be notified specifically before the Goalkeeper is changed whether the change is made by means of another player on the field or by means of a substitute from the sideline. When the Goalkeeper is changed between quarters, the referees need not be notified.

When all players of a team have completed their required playing time, the team has achieved "free substitution" status. For the remainder of the game, that team may substitute any number of players: On a goal kick, after a goal, during any extended time out (as for an injury), between quarters, and, by the team in possession, on a throw-in.

A player arriving late before or after the team has achieved "free substitution", must play the required personal time, or the remainder of the game. The "free substitution" status continues for the other players.

> PENALTY: For illegal substitution, an indirect kick shall be awarded to the opposing team if the infraction is noted while the ball is in play, from the sport of the ball at that time. Whether or not the ball is in play, the entering player shall be cautioned.

Law Four — PLAYERS EQUIPMENT

A player shall not wear anything which is dangerous to himself or herself, or to another player. Players in all divisions shall wear gym, tennis, molded soccer shoes, or shoes with screw-in cleats. Metal or metal-tipped cleats are not allowed. The maximum length of a cleat is ¾", the minimum width is ½" if individually mounted. If molded, and there are 10 or more cleats, the maximum length is ¾" and the minimum width is 3/8".

The following shall be considered as illegal equipment, and as such shall not be worn by any player:

a. Shin guards with exposed sharp edges.

b. Face or spectacle guards, helmets of any kind. Soft headwear, such as knit caps, are permitted. The goalkeeper is permitted to wear a soft-billed cap.

c. Knee, head, thigh or hip pads containing sole leather, fibre, metal or and dangerous material, even though covered with soft padding.

d. Any cast of any type, even though covered with soft padding.

e. A knee brace may be worn, but shall be wrapped, and shall be approved by the referees.

f. Cleats with sharp edges.

g. **Players shall not have any foreign objects in their mouths, such as gum or ice. Teeth guards are permitted.**

These rules shall not be waived even by agreement between both coaches and the referees.

All players on a team must wear shirts of the same identifying color. The Goalkeeper must wear a color different than that of either team.

It is the responsibility of the home team to change to a different color, if the two teams normally wear the same color.

Numbers of shirts are required, and must be different (. . . for each player), however, for non-tournament games when a team, because of a color conflict must wear alternate shirts, such shirts need not be numbered.

> PENALTY: If a player is wearing dangerous or illegal equipment, participation is forbidden until this is corrected, to the satisfaction of the referee.
>
> **For an unresolved color conflict, the referees may permit the game to proceed, but the incident must be reported to the District Representative.**

Law Five — THE REFEREE

There shall be **two referees,** with equal jurisdiction. A single referee may be used in an emergency situation, with linesmen to assist only by indicating "out-of-bounds." Both referees shall have equal authority and responsibility in the calling of fouls and violations on any part of the field at any time.

The authority and the exercise of powers granted to referees by the Laws of the Game commence as soon as they enter the field of play. The power of penalizing shall extend to offenses committed when play has been temporarily suspended, or the ball is out of play. (A free kick may not be awarded if the ball is out of play when a foul is committed, but players may be cautioned or ejected.)

A referee's decision on points of fact connected with the play shall be final.

The Referee shall:

a. Enforce the laws.

b. Refrain from penalizing in cases where doing so would give an advantage to the offending team.

c. Act as game timekeeper, unless provision has been made by League or Tournament officials for sideline timekeeping. Time lost through accident or unusual delay is to be added.

d. Have the authority to stop the game for an infringement of the Laws, and to suspend or terminate the game if weather conditions or actions of spectators or players indicate that the stoppage is necessary. Such stoppage and the reasons therefore should be reported to the league administrator.

e. Caution any player guilty of misconduct, and eject the player if this is repeated. Ejections should be reported to the league administrator.

f. Allow no one other than the active players and linesmen to enter the field without permission.

g. Stop the game if a player is injured, but not during a drive on goal unless the injury appears to be serious. (The nearest referee is obliged to quickly check the condition of the injured player.) The referee only need have reason to believe that a player is seriously injured to stop the game, even if there is a drive on goal.

h. Eject any player who is guilty of violent conduct, serious foul play, or the use of abusive language.

i. Signal for the re-starting of the game after any stoppage. For the taking of kicks, the signal in passers and wings must be with the whistle. For other divisions, the common practice throughout the world of allowing the kick to be taken as soon as the ball is properly placed, without a whistle, is to be followed. The referee may delay such a "quick" kick at his or her discretion. A second whistle may be given after a substitution, an extended time out, or for the taking of a penalty kick.

j. Use drop ball to restart game, after unresolved referee decisions, such as a whistle blown by mistake, or unknown team last touches out of bounds ball.

NOTES:

1. **A referee may reverse a decision as long as play has not been restarted.**

2. **If the "advantage" clause has been applied, this decision cannot be revoked if the advantage is not realized.**

3. **Games may not be forfeited by referees. Conditions indicating a possible forfeit must be reported to the District Representative for a decision.**

4. **If a player or two players on the same team simultaneously commits two infringements, one of which calls for an indirect kick, and the other of which calls for a direct kick, a direct kick shall be awarded.**

5. **Coaching from the touchline during the course of the game shall be limited to verbal communication with the players of the coach's team. Megaphones, bullhorns, etc., may not be used. No coaching or comments shall be directed to the players or coaches of the opposing team.**

6. **During the course of the game, all coaches must remain on the side of the field, between the center line and the top of the penalty area (18 yd. line) where the team's substitutes are situated.**

   PENALTY: For violation of Law Five notes 5 or 6 — After receiving one caution, the offending coach shall be ejected from the playing field.

Law Six — LINESMEN

The duties of linesmen shall be limited to indicating to the referee when a ball goes out-of-bounds.

Law Seven — DURATION OF THE GAME

All games will be played in quarters with a kick-off to begin each quarter. The team that kicks off in the 1st quarter will kick off in the 3rd quarter. The team that kicks off in the 2nd quarter will kick off in the 4th quarter. Teams will change ends at the end of each quarter. Times of quarters will be:

Passers (6, 7)	10 minutes
Wings and Strikers (8-11)	15 minutes
Kickers, Minors and Seniors (12-18)	20 minutes

Intervals between quarters will be one minutes; half time interval will be 10 minutes.

Allowances shall be made within each period for time lost through accident or other cause, the amount of which shall be at the discretion of the referee. This time may not be added to a different period.

Time shall be extended only to permit the taking of a penalty-kick which was awarded before time ran out. Time may not be extended for the taking of other free kicks.

Play ends exactly at the instant that time runs out, regardless of the position or motion of the ball at that time.

Law Eight — THE START OF PLAY

At the beginning of the game, choice of ends and the kick-off shall be decided by the toss of a coin. The team winning the toss shall choose an end or the kick-off, the team losing the toss will receive the remaining choice.

Upon the referee's signal, the game is started by a player taking a placekick (i.e. a kick at the ball while it is stationary on the ground at mid-field) into the opponent's half of the field. The players of each team must be in their team's half of the field until the ball is kicked. Opposing players must remain 10 yards from the ball until it is kicked.

As in all free kicks, the ball is not in play until it has travelled the distance of its own circumference, and the kicker may not play the ball a second time until it has been touched by another player, of either team.

For violation of the above provisions, the kick must be re-taken, except for the case where the kicker plays the ball a second time, the kick-off otherwise having been legal. In that case, an indirect kick is awarded to the opposing team.

A goal may not be scored direct from a kick-off.

After a goal has been scored, the game is re-started in a like manner, by the team scored against.

After a game has been stopped while the ball was in play, as for an injury, it is re-started with a drop ball. The referee shall drop the ball where it was when play was stopped, and it shall be in play when it touches the ground. If the ball was in play within a penalty area and not in possession of the goalkeeper when the stoppage occurred, it shall be dropped at the nearest point outside the penalty area. If the ball was in clear possession of the goalkeeper when the stoppage occurred, play will be re-started with an indirect free kick taken by the goalkeeper's team at the place where it was when the stoppage occurred, and in accordance with Law 13.

In the Passers division, a kick taken under these circumstances will be taken from a point 12 yards from the goal line if the ball was not at least 12 yards from the goal line when the stoppage occurred.

Law Nine — BALL IN AND OUT OF PLAY

The ball is out of play when it has completely crossed the goal-line or touchline, whether on the ground or in the air, and when the game has been stopped by the referee.

The ball is in play at all other times, including:

1. If it rebounds onto the field from a goal-post, crossbar or corner flag.

2. If it strikes the referee or linesman on the field of play.

3. If there is an apparent infringement, but no signal has been given by the referee.

Law Ten — METHOD OF SCORING

Except as otherwise provided by these Laws, a goal is scored when the whole of the ball has passed over the goal-line, between the goal-posts, and under the crossbar.

A goal is not allowed if the ball has been thrown, carried, or intentionally propelled by hand or arm by a player of the attacking team, other than the attacking team's goalie throwing from his own penalty area.

The team scoring more goals shall be the winner; if there are no goals, or an equal number of goals are scored by each team, the game shall be a draw.

NOTES:

1. A goal may not be allowed if the ball has not crossed the goal-line. If the ball is stopped by an outside agency (i.e., a dog, or spectator), it must be dropped, at the nearest point outside the penalty area.

2. The referee must not award a goal unless in a position to observe and be certain that the ball has completely crossed the goal-line.

3. A goal may not be allowed if the ball touches a foreign agency before entering the goal (dog, spectator, etc.). The referee is not a foreign agency.

Law Eleven — OFF-SIDE

A player is off-side if nearer the opponent's goal-line than the ball at the moment the ball is played toward the player by a team-mate, unless:

1. The player is in his or her own half of the field of play.

2. There are at least two opponents nearer to their goal-line.

3. The ball is received directly from a goal-kick, corner-kick, throw-in or drop ball.

PENALTY: An indirect free-kick by the opposing team, from the place where the infringement occurred, unless the offense is committed by a player in the opponents' goal area, in which case, the free kick shall be taken from a point anywhere within that half of the goal area in which the offense occurred (or 12-yard line for Passers).

NOTE: It is stressed that off-side is determined at the instant the ball is passed by a team-mate to the player in an off-side position. The position of the player when the ball is received has no bearing on off-side.

A player in an off-side position shall not be penalized unless interfering with the play or with an opponent, or able to gain an advantage by being in an off-side position.

1. CLEAR PASS TO ONE ON SAME SIDE

(A) has run the ball up, and having (D) in front passes to (B). (B) is off-side because he is in front of (A) and there are not two opponents between him and goal-line when the ball is passed by (A).

If (B) waits for (E) to fall back before he shoots, this will not put him on-side, because it does not alter his position with relation to (A) at the moment the ball was passed by (A).

B is Off-Side

2. CLEAR PASS TO ONE OF SAME SIDE

(Continued)

(A) has run the ball up, and having (D) in front passes across the field. (B) runs from position 1 to position 2. (B) is not off-side because at the moment the ball was passed by (A) he was not in front of the ball, and had two opponents between him and the goal-line.

B is Not Off-Side

146

3. CLEAR PASS TO ONE OF SAME SIDE
(Continued)

(A) and (B) make a passing run up the wing. (A) passes the ball to (B) who can not shoot because he has (D) in front. (A) then runs from position 1 to position 2 at which time (B) passes the ball to him. (A) is off-side because he is in front of the ball and he had not two opponents between him and the goal-line when the ball was played by (B).

A is Off-Side

4. RUNNING BACK FOR BALL

(A) centers the ball. (B) runs back from position 1 to position 2, and then dribbles between (D) and (E) and scores. (B) is off-side because he is in front of the ball and he had not two opponents between him and the goal-line at the moment the ball was played by (A).

B is Off-Side

5. RUNNING BACK FOR BALL
(Continued)

(A) makes a high shot at goal, and the wind and screw carry the ball back. (B) runs from position 1 to position 2 and scores. (B) is off-side because he is in front of the ball and he had not two opponents between him and the goal-line at the moment the ball was last played by (A).

B is Off-Side

147

6. SHOT AT GOAL RETURNED BY GOALKEEPER

(A) shoots at goal. The ball is played by (C) and (B) obtains possession but slips and passes the ball to (F) who scores. (F) is off-side because he is in front of (B), and when the ball was passed by (B) he had not two opponents between him and the goal-line.

F is Off-Side

7. BALL REBOUNDING FROM GOAL-POSTS OR CROSS-BAR

(A) shoots for goal and the ball rebounds from the goal-post into play. (B) secures the ball and scores. (B) is off-side because the ball is last played by (A), a player of his own side, and when (A) played it (B) was in front of the ball and did not have two opponents between him and the goal-line.

B is Off-Side

8. BALL REBOUNDING FROM GOAL-POSTS OR CROSS-BAR

(A) shoots for goal and the ball rebounds from the cross-bar into play. (A) follows up from position 1 to position 2, and then passes to (B) who has run up on the other side. (B) is off-side because the ball is last played by (a), a player of his own side, and when (A) played it (B) was in front of the ball and did not have two opponents between him and the goal-line. If (A) had scored himself at the second attempt, instead of passing to (B), it would have been a goal.

B is Off-Side

148

9. OBSTRUCTING THE GOALKEEPER

(A) shoots for goal and scores. (B) however, obstructs (C) so that he cannot get at the ball. The goal must be disallowed, because (B) is in an off-side position and may not touch the ball himself, nor in any way whatever interfere with an opponent.

B is Off-Side

10. OBSTRUCTING THE GOALKEEPER
(Continued)

(A) shoots for goal. (B) runs from position 2 to position 1 while the ball is in transit and prevents (C) from playing it properly. (B) is off-side because he is in front of (A) and has not two opponents between him and the goal-line when (A) plays the ball. When in this position (B) may not touch the ball himself, nor in any way whatever interfere with an opponent.

B is Off-Side

11. OBSTRUCTING AN OPPONENT OTHER THAN THE GOALKEEPER

(A) shoots for goal. (B) prevents (E) from running in to intercept the ball. (B) is off-side because he is in front of (A) and has not two opponents between him and the goal-line when (A) plays the ball. When in this position (B) may not touch the ball himself, nor in any way whatever interfere with an opponent.

B is Off-Side

12. AFTER A CORNER-KICK

(A) takes a corner-kick and the ball goes to (B). (B) shoots for goal and as the ball is passing through, (F) deflects it into the goal. (F) is off-side because after the corner-kick has been taken the ball is last played by (B), a player of his own side, and when (B) played it (F) was in front of the ball and has not two opponents between him and the goal-line.

F is Off-Side

13. AFTER A CORNER-KICK

(Continued)

(A) takes a corner-kick and the ball goes to (B), who puts it through goal. (B) has only one opponent between him and goal-line, but he is not off-side because a player cannot be off-side directly from a corner-kick.

B is Not Off-Side

14. AFTER A CORNER-KICK

(Continued)

(A) takes a corner-kick and (D) attempts to kick it upfield, but miskicks and the ball goes to (B), who puts it through goal. (B) is not off-side because the ball was last played by an opponent, (D).

B is Not Off-Side

15. AFTER A THROW-IN FROM THE TOUCHLINE

(A) throws to (B) and then runs from touchline to position (A2). (B) passes the ball to (A) in position 2. (A) is off-side because he is in front of the ball and has not two opponents between him and the goal-line when the ball is passed forward to him by (B).

A is Off-Side

16. AFTER A THROW-IN FROM THE TOUCH-LINE (Continued)

(A) throws the ball to (B). Although (B) is in front of the ball and has not two opponents between him and the goal-line, he is not off-side because a player cannot be off-side from a throw-in.

B is Not Off-Side

17. A PLAYER CANNOT PUT HIMSELF ON-SIDE BY RUNNING BACK INTO HIS OWN HALF OF THE FIELD OF PLAY.

If (A) is in his opponents' half of the field of play, and is off-side in position when (B) last played the ball, he cannot put himself on-side by moving back into his own half of the field of play.

A is Off-Side

151

18. A PLAYER WITHIN HIS OWN HALF OF THE FIELD OF PLAY IS NOT OFF-SIDE WHEN HE ENTERS HIS OPPONENTS HALF OF THE FIELD OF PLAY.

If (A) is in his own half of the field of play he is on-side, although he is in front of the ball and there are not two opponents nearer their own goal-line when (B) last played the ball. (A) is therefore not off-side when he enters his opponents' half of the field of play.

A is Not Off-Side

Law Twelve — FOULS, AND MISCONDUCT

The intentional commission of any of the following offenses will result in the award of a direct free kick to the opposing team, at the point of the offense, **unless the offense is committed by a player in the opponents' goal area, in which case, the free kick shall be taken from a point anywhere within that half of the goal area in which the offense occurred (or 12-yard line for passers).** If the offense be by a member of the defending team within its own penalty area, a penalty kick will be awarded.

These penalties may be awarded only if the ball was in play at the time of the offense, but the position of the ball is irrelevant, except, of course, in the case of handball:

1. Kicking or attempting to kick an opponent.
2. Tripping or attempted tripping, with leg or body.
3. Jumping at an opponent.
4. Charging an opponent from behind.
5. Striking or attempting to strike an opponent.
6. Holding an opponent.
7. Pushing an opponent, with hand or arm.
8. Charges an opponent in a violent or dangerous manner. (A fair charge requires that both players have at least one foot on the ground, and that contact be shoulder-to-shoulder).
9. **Carries, strikes or propels the ball with hand or arm, (except for a goalkeeeeper within his or her own penalty area). Girls may protect their chests from the impact of the ball by holding their arms against their chest, but any movement of the arm towards the ball will be called a "handball."**
10. Charging a goalkeeper in the goal area or where goalkeeper is in possession of the ball in penalty area.

11. A sliding tackle made from outside the peripheral vision of the opponent in possession of the ball (the rear 180 degrees) will be considered tripping, even if first contact is with the ball. If no contact is made with either player or ball, it will be called "dangerous play", with an indirect kick awarded.

12. Attempting to kick a ball while in possession of the goalkeeper. Possession is having control, even if only with one hand.

> NOTE: Charging of the goalkeeper in the goal area or in possession of the ball, or attempting to kick a ball in the goalkeeper's possession must be punished by a caution or ejection, the choice to be subject to the referee's judgment.

The commission of any of the following offenses will result in the award of an indirect free kick, taken by the opposing team at the point of infringement:

1. Playing in a manner which could result in injury to the player or to any other player. Examples of dangerous play are: (a) raising the foot, in an attempt to play the ball, to the level of an opponent's chest or higher when the opponent is in a normal position; or (b) using a double kick (scissors, bicycle, or hitch kick) within six feet of an opponent; or (c) lowering the head to the level of the waist or lower in an attempt to head the ball in the presence of an oncoming player; or (d) playing or attempting to play the ball while lying on the ground within six feet of an opponent. "Dangerous Play" is always a judgment call, which is made at the discretion of the referee, These examples are not exclusive. They are for illustration only and are not meant to limit the use of discretion by the referee.

2. Charging fairly when the ball is not within playing distance of the players concerned.

3. When not playing the ball, interposing the body so as to obstruct an opponent's movement.

4. Improper clearing of the ball by the Goalkeeper. The following rules shall apply:

Passers and Wings: **Passer and Wing Goalkeepers may run with the ball and take any number of steps while inside the penalty area, as long as there is no excessive delay in clearing the ball.**

Strikers Kickers Minors and Seniors: **Striker, Kicker, Minor, and Senior Goalkeepers may not take more than four steps while in clear possession before releasing the ball so that it is played by another player. "Clear Possession" shall include holding, bouncing or throwing the ball in the air and catching it.**

5. Excessive delay in clearing the ball by the goalkeeper.

A player who enters or leaves the field without the referee's permission shall be cautioned. If the game is stopped to administer this caution, the game will be re-started by an indirect kick taken by the opposing team at the point where this player was when the game was stopped, or where the offense was committed.

A caution shall be administered also:

1.   If a player persistently infringes the Laws of the Game.

2.   If dissent is shown by word or action with any decision of the referee.

A caution may be administered for:

1.   Unsportsmanlike conduct.

2.   Foul language.

These also require that an indirect kick be awarded to the opposing team from the point of the offense.

A player will be ejected from the game for:

1.   Violent conduct or serious foul play.

2.   The use of abusive language.

3.   A second offense requiring a caution.

If the game is stopped to eject the player, no other Law having been infringed, an indirect kick shall be awarded to the opposing team from the point of the offense.

NOTE:

1.   If a goalkeeper throws the ball vigorously, at an opponent, or pushed with the ball while holding it, the referee shall award a penalty-kick, provided that the offense took place in the penalty area.

2.   The referee need not stop the game to administer a caution: the advantage clause may be invoked. The caution will be administered as soon as play stops.

3.   An attempt to prevent a throw-in being taken or to prevent the goalkeeper from clearing the ball in unsportsmanlike conduct.

4.   All players are subject to these Laws, whether on or off the field, and whether playing or substitutes.

Law Thirteen — FREE KICK

There are two types of free kicks: Direct from which a goal can be scored direct against the offending team and indirect, from which a goal cannot be scored unless the ball has been touched after the kick by any other player, of either team, before it enters the goal.

When a free kick is being taken by a defending team from inside its own penalty area, all opposing players must be outside the penalty area and at least 10 yards from the ball. To be in play, the ball must travel the distance of its own circumference and beyond the penalty area. It may not be kicked back to the goalkeeper to be cleared. A free kick which does not pass beyond the penalty area must be retaken.

Any free kick awarded to a defending team inside its own goal area may be taken from any point within that half of the goal area in which the free kick has been awarded **(or 12-yard line for Passers).**

When a free kick is being taken outside the kicker's own penalty area, it may be kicked in any direction. Players of the opposing team should be 10 yards from the ball and must be at least 10 yards from the ball if requested by the kicker or referee, except in the case of an indirect kick being taken within less than 10 yards of the opponent's goal. In this case, defending players may stand on the goal-line, between the goal-posts. On all free kicks, the ball is not in play until it has travelled the distance of its own circumference.

If players of the opposing side encroach into the penalty area, or within 10 yards of the ball, the referee may delay the taking of the kick until the Law is complied with.

Encroachment is to be treated as unsportsmanlike conduct.

The ball must be stationary when the kick is taken, and the kicker may not play the ball again until it has been touched by another player.

PENALTY: For playing the ball twice, an indirect kick is awarded to the opposing team at the point where it was played the second time.

For delaying the taking of a kick by encroachment or attempts at distracting the kicker, a caution shall be given.

Law Fourteen — PENALTY KICK

A penalty-kick is taken from the penalty mark, which is opposite the center of the goal and 12 yards from the goal-line.

When the kick is taken, all players other than the player taking the kick and the opposing goalkeeper, shall be within the field of play but outside the penalty area, and at least 10 yards from the ball.

The goalkeeper must stand on the goal-line, between the goal-posts, and may not lift or slide either foot until the ball is kicked. Movement of the body or arms is permitted.

The kick must be forward, and may not be played a second time by the kicker until touched by another player. The ball must travel the distance of its circumference before it is in play. A goal may be scored direct from a penalty kick.

If necessary, time of play shall be extended at the end of any quarter to allow a penalty-kick to be taken. If, in such a case, the ball touches the goalkeeper before passing completely over the goal-line and into the goal, the goal is valid. If it rebounds onto the field or out of bounds, whether from the goal or the goalkeeper, time expires at once.

PENALTY: 1. For any infringement of this Law by the defending team, the kick is retaken if a goal is not scored. Goal is allowed if scored.

2. For any infringement of this Law by the attacking team, the kick is retaken if a goal is scored. If a

goal is not scored and the ball out of play, continue the game as is normal. However, if the goalkeeper deflects the ball out of bounds, or if it rebounds into play, play is stopped and an indirect kick is awarded to the defending team.

3. If the kicker is guilty of an infringement after the ball is in play, play is stopped and an indirect kick is awarded to the defending team.

4. If both teams infringe, the kick is retaken whether or not it scored.

NOTES:

1. The penalty-kick may not be taken until the signal to do so is given by the referee. This signal will not be given until all players are in position in accordance with the Law.

2. The kick shall be taken even if an infringement is noted by the referee after giving the signal for the kick. A decision will then be made in accordance with the Law, depending on the outcome of the kick.

Law Fifteen — THROW-IN

When the whole of the ball has passed over the touchline, either on the ground or in the air, it shall be put into play by a throw-in in any direction at the point where it crossed the line, by a player of the team opposite to that of the player who last touched it.

The thrower at the moment of delivering the ball must face the field of play with both feet outside the touchline and part of each foot in contact with the ground. The thrower shall use both hands equally and shall deliver the ball from behind and over his head. The ball shall be in play immediately as it enters the field of play, but the thrower shall not again play the ball until it has been touched by another player.

A goal may not be scored direct from a throw-in.

The offside law does not apply at the taking of a throw-in.

PENALTY: 1. For an improper throw-in, it shall be taken by the other team.

2. For playing the ball a second time, an indirect kick by the opposing team at the point of the offense.

Law Sixteen — GOAL KICK

When the ball passes completely over the defending team's goal line, and was last touched by an attacking player, and a goal was not scored, it is put into play by an indirect kick by the defending team, taken from a point within that half of the goal area nearest to where it crossed the line. **In the Passers Division the kick may be taken from in front of the goal area, up to 12 yards from the Goal Line.**

All provisions of the Laws regarding free kicks from a defending team's penalty area apply, except that the off-side Law does not apply at the taking of the kick.

Law Seventeen — CORNER KICK

When the ball passes completely over the defending team's goal line, and was last touched by a defending player, and a goal has not scored, it is put into play by a direct kick, taken by a player of the attacking team from the corner of the field nearest to where the ball crossed the line. The ball must be placed within the quarter circle, or no more than one yard from both the touchline and goal line.

The corner flag may not be moved for the taking of the corner-kick. A goal may be scored direct from a corner-kick.

Defending players must remain 10 yards from the ball until it is in play, that is has travelled the distance of its own circumference. The kicker may not play the ball a second time until it has been touched by another player.

The off-side Law does not apply at the taking of the kick.

PENALTY: For playing the ball a second time, an indirect kick will be awarded the defending team at the point of the offense.

glossary of soccer terms

CENTER CIRCLE: The circle with a ten-yard radius at the middle of the field.

CHIP: To loft a pass by striking the ball at the lowest possible point.

CLEAR: Moving the ball up the field out of scoring range — usually a long pass.

CORNER KICK: A direct free kick taken by the attacking team from the one-yard arc at the corner of the field after the ball goes over the goal line having last been touched by a defending player.

COVER: To take up a position close to an opponent to challenge his efforts. Also, to take up a position close to a teammate to provide support.

CROSS: A pass from one side of the field to either the center or the other side of the field.

DEPTH: Support either in defense or attack.

DIRECT FREE KICK: A kick awarded on a personal foul which can score directly from the kicker's foot.

DRIBBLING: To move the ball along the ground using the feet while keeping the ball under control.

DROP BALL: A means used by the referee to put the ball back into play after a temporary suspension of play when neither team is awarded possession of the ball.

FEINTING: A deceptive move made by a player in order to dupe an opponent.

FIRST-TIME: Striking a ball immediately without first bringing it under control.

GOAL AREA: The area directly in front of the goal, six yards x twelve yards, from which all goal kicks are taken.

GOAL KICK: An indirect free kick taken by the defensive team after the ball goes out of bounds over the goal line having last been touched by an attacking player. The kick is taken from anywhere within the half of the goal area closer to where the ball went out of bounds.

GOAL-LINE: The out-of-bounds line at each end of the field.

HALF-VOLLEY: Playing the ball the instant it starts to bounce up after hitting the ground.

HEADING: The technique of hitting the ball with the head, usually the forehead.

INDIRECT FREE KICK: A free kick which cannot score a goal unless touched by one other player besides the one taking the kick.

JOCKEYING: Containing an opponent, and sometimes giving ground, while waiting for an opportunity to challenge for the ball.

KICKOFF: The starting of play from the middle of the field at the beginning of each period and after a goal has been scored.

MARKING: To guard an opponent.

MOBILITY: Movement by players in order to utilize existing space and create new space to develop passing opportunities.

OBSTRUCTION: Impeding an opponent's movement by remaining in his direct path.

OFFSIDE POSITION: When a player is ahead of the ball while the ball is being played by a member of his team unless: (1) he is in his own half of the field, (2) there are two opponents nearer their own goal than he is, (3) the ball is touched by an opponent or (4) he receives the ball directly from a corner kick, goal kick, throw-in or drop ball.

OFFSIDES: A player who is in an offside position when the ball is played to him or one who is in an offside position and is seeking to gain an attacking advantage.

PENALTY AREA: The area, 18 yards x 44 yards, in front of the goal where the goalkeeper is permitted to use his hands.

PENALTY KICK: A free kick awarded the attacking team after a defending player commits a personal foul within his penalty area. The kick is taken from a spot 12 yards in front of the goal and no player except the kicker and the goalkeeper, who must be stationary with both feet on the goal line, may be within the penalty area until the kick is taken.

SAVE: The deflection or catching of a ball by the goalkeeper to prevent a goal.

STRIKER: A central attacking forward.

SWEEPER: A free back behind the last line of defenders.

TACKLING: Technique used to dispossess an opponent of the ball.

THROW-IN: The means of putting the ball back into play after it goes out of bounds over the touchline.

TOUCHLINE: The side boundaries of the field.

TRAPPING: Bringing the ball under control and stopping it.

WING: A forward who generally positions himself and plays near the side boundaries of the field.

SPORTS PUBLICATIONS
by
THE ATHLETIC INSTITUTE

is backed by 48 years of promoting the advancement of sports, physical education, health, recreation and dance in America.

If you want the very best — the most up-to-date information written by leading authorities — graphic illustrations — line drawings — sequential photos and educationally sound, consider the following titles:

Archery	Pathfinder (Backpacking)
Badminton	Power Volleyball, The Woman's Game
Basketball	Basketball, The Woman's Game
On The Lesson Tee	Health Care and the Female Athlete
Run America	A Manual for Women's Self-Defense
Soccer	Modern Women's Gymnastics
Tennis Your Way	Softball, Fast and Slo Pitch
Racquetball 1-2-3	Touch and Flag Football Rules
Modern Athletic Training	Track & Field for Men and Women

Coaches Edition:
Youth League Baseball
Youth League Basketball
Youth League Football
Youth League Ice Hockey
Youth League Soccer
Youth League Softball
Youth League Wrestling

For Information On Obtaining These Books Write To:
The Athletic Institute
Publications Department
200 Castlewood Drive
North Palm Beach, FL 33408